MW00439796

"I want You to Love ME"

Sue Smith

Copyright © 2019 Sue Smith
All rights reserved.
ISBN: 9781087468723

Dedicated to:
God, the director of my life and to,
Jim, my soul mate, best friend and lover,
and to my children, my reason for living.

Encouraged by:
Deb Russell and
Lee Parmenter

Introduction

Blessed are they, which hunger and thirst after righteousness: for they shall be filled.
Matthew 5:6

I'm not ready to be turned out to pasture yet, but I can see it coming on the horizon. I am still able to enjoy my life style, though with less endurance, speed or agility. I'm still able to ride my horse, hike, camp and tend my rose garden. I am only reminded of my age when looking at my cousin's faces. I am startled to realize my true and best friends are starting to look a little worn around the edges. Then there are the not so gentle reminders from a grandchild when astonishingly he exclaims, "Gee, I didn't know old grandmothers can run." Or when a blessed granddaughter surprises me by saying, "You're getting old and wrinkled aren't you Grandma." Then goes on to reassure me by saying, "It is O.K. Grandma, because what I love about you is on the inside."

I've been looking back a lot lately, analyzing, remembering, amazed. Shaking my head, I ask my Lord, "How did I get here." I recall the first time I ever heard His voice. I had ridden my horse out on the west side of our ranch to my secret place. In the hollow of three hills is a low grassy place. I climbed off my horse and laid on my back, looking up at the clear blue sky. I asked,

i

"Lord, what do you want me to be when I grow up?" In my young mind I'm expecting a famous singer or champion horsewoman – something really exceptional – I lay there for quite a period of time – let my mind settle into nothingness and then, clearly heard. "I want you to love Me."

This is my story of a dyslexic little girl, and why at a very young age she realized that nothing in her being was enough to engineer a productive, purposeful life on her own. Her hunger and thirst for righteousness turned her problematic journey into a victorious ride.

Chapter 1

Growing up on Carmen Creek

I will lift mine eyes to the mountains, from whence cometh my strength, my strength cometh from the Lord who made the heavens and the earth.
Psalms 121:1

Growing up on Carmen Creek and being a part of the McFarland family gives a person a broad, firm foundation. Carmen Creek is located in Lemhi County, Idaho. It is a beautiful ranching community that sits at the base of the Bitterroot Mountains. The mountains rise up from the valley floor 10,000 feet. Their rough, rugged edges stand stately, salted most months with snow. I asked my nine years old granddaughter to explain the beauty of the place we call home. She said, "It is like living in a dream, but it is real."

Our valley is about seven miles long with the creek rushing down the center. Large cottonwood, aspen, birch, and willows follow the stream. The benches along the creek are pasture land and the higher land, hay meadows. All kept green, by the hard work of many and the abundant supply of water from Carmen Creek. The large hay fields are surrounded by sagebrush hills. These hills come alive in the spring with

1

buttercups, yellow bells, blue bells, lupine, larkspur and balsam root. Then above the hills, our magnificent mountains.

Our ranch on Carmen Creek was purchased in 1924 by my grandparents Peter and Gudrun McFarland. The story of Grandpa buying this ranch is fun family history. The story goes like this. Grandpa had a cousin that already lived in Lemhi County, Curley McFarland. In a visit one day Curley told Grandpa about a ranch for sale up Carmen Creek. My Grandparents were living in Poplar, Idaho 180 miles from Carmen. One fall day, Curley and Grandpa Pete went to visit a realtor in Idaho Falls, Idaho. They all traveled to Carmen to see the ranch. One the spot, Grandpa said, "I'll take it!" Grandpa arrived home and let his wife and six children know they were moving to Carmen, and soon. I wonder if he took the time to explain that Carmen may be beautiful but is a rural, isolated community. It is twelve miles to the only grocery store. For major shopping or doctoring you either travel 150 miles to Missoula, Montana or 150 miles to Idaho Falls, Idaho. Either direction you have to go over 7,000+ foot passes. Perhaps this was best left unsaid.

The ranch was bought from the Becker family and their son Jack, age 22, came to Poplar to help move Grandpa's sheep. My Uncle Dave, age 17 and my Uncle Arch age 15 were given the responsibility to move the 1,500 sheep through the high mountain desert 180 miles to their new home in Carmen. They had a team pulling a camp wagon and two saddle horse. I can imagine this was a great adventure for these independent, hardworking young boys, that is until the water ran low, the sheep grew weary of travel and weather began to turn sour. When they reached Birch Creek the fun had worn thin and survival was their main concern. They had eaten nothing but mutton and sourdough bread the entire trip. At Birch creek they were able to catch a few fish and kill a duck. This is the way Uncle Arch celebrated his 16th birthday on December 6th. They had to go over Gilmore summit, 7,200 ft high, where the wind blows endlessly and either carries sand or snow. Over the pass the weather turned bitter and dropped to 35 below zero, and they still had 70 miles before reaching the ranch. Bedraggled, frost bitten and beyond weary they reach their new home on Christmas eve, 1924.

Grandpa and the rest of the family were there to meet them but they had had an adventure of their own. Peter, Gudrun, Katie, Harold, Mary and Glen made the trip on the Gilmore and Pittsburg train. I remember Aunt Katie telling and retelling the story. They left Idaho Falls and thought they would get to Leadore that day. Around Grant, Montana the train had to stop so the crew could pry frozen varmints off the track. It was determined the train could not make the trip and they were put into a nine-passenger automobile, called the Gallopin Goose. The car was loaded and ready to head over Bannock Pass, it was snowing and cold but as the story goes, they all got to warm up because the car could not make it over the divide and they all had to get out and push.

These stories, of the arrival of the McFarland's to Carmen Creek, are told and retold, passed down the five generations of McFarland's enjoying the fruitful valley of Carmen Creek.

By 1949, Pete McFarland's children all had their own ranches up and down the Carmen valley. We are a large clan and very dependent on each other for the hard work encountered in running the multiple ranches plus we receive emotional and social strength from each other. Many of our traditions have been in existence for 94 years. Can you imagine the Christmas Eve celebration Grandma Gudrun had ready for her travel weary family that first year in their new home?

The first Christmas eve I can remember was when I was 4 years old. We were in Grandma Gudrun's old two-story ranch house. The home was abuzz with 50 or so McFarland's all talking at the same time. The Christmas tree was in the corner of the living room and was decorated with lights that bubbled. Under the tree were packages of every shape and size. After a fine dinner we were all seated in the living room and names were called out one at a time and we each received a gift. What a sense of belonging, a sense of warmth, a sense of joint love. I now carry on the 94-year-old tradition. I invite the clan to my home and try to fill it with as much warmth and love as my Grandmother did.

Coffee time was every day at 4:00 P.M. Men came in out of the fields, kids from their play and the women served coffee and goodies. It was time to connect, a time to talk about the next day's work, the cattle market, or the next social event. It was a time for the women to sit down and visit for a period of time. We all worked hard, we all got up early and worked until the last cow was milked in the evening, but the women, their work was truly never done. As kids coming home from school on the bus, we would start looking for which aunt or uncle's house had a group of cars parked around it. As soon as we spotted them, we would all pile off the bus and run to coffee time, leaving the bus virtually empty. An interesting side-note. My grandparents belonged to the LDS church. Grandma came from Norway as a little girl, and she loved her coffee. I remember her saying, "Well, I was Norwegian before I was Mormon, I will always love my coffee!"

Halloween on Carmen Creek was totally different than Halloween today. Never was a dime spent on costumes and so typically we were either cowboys or Indians. My favorite memories of Halloween center around Aunt Norma, she knew how to have fun. She would dress up in some terrifying outfit and 8 or 10 of us cousins would load up in her car and head down the valley. We would stop at each ranch, pile out of the car, and start yelling trick or treat. We were always greeted as if we were the terrors of the community, fake fear and trepidation. Then our aunt or uncle would invite us in for hot chocolate and fresh baked cookies. Through loud laughter and thanks, we would tear out of that house, load up in the car, to head to our next destination. Down the creek we went; homemade popcorn balls, polished apples, homemade candy or even a cherished orange. I still hear the laughter, the phony fear but mostly the feeling of us pleasing our aunts and uncles and how their welcome filled my heart.

When the McFarland's first came to Carmen, they were sheep people. Through the years as the wool prices began to dwindle, they started buying cattle. In my early memories all the families still had hundreds of sheep. Now sheep are interesting animals one has to learn to love. This love is tested during shearing time. Towards the end of May when the nights are no longer so cold the shearing crew came to Lemhi, County. You would set up a date for them to come to your ranch and again the whole family emerges to help with the hot, not so pleasant-smelling business of shearing hundreds of sheep. Each person has their job. Some gather the sheep into the corrals, others work the sheep up a narrow alleyway, someone else catches a sheep by a front foot and drags it to a shearer. The shearer grabs the sheep and sets it on its butt and turns it, so its back is against the shearer's legs. He grabs his electric clippers, that are dangling down in front of him, and holding the sheep's head up, makes a long swipe from her lower belly up to her chin. From that start he continues to make long, smooth glides and can finish a sheep in a matter of minutes. Someone else gathers the fleece and ties it with a long string. In order to fill the fleece sacks with as many fleeces as possible they had to be stomped into the sacks. Each ranch had a fleece bag platform. It was about 8 or 10 feet tall and had a flat top with a round hole in the middle. You would put the sack through the hole and place a ring around the top to hold the fleece sack in place. The sack is suspended and hangs limply in midair. So, the story goes, because children have small feet, they were best fit for the job of stomping the fleeces in the sack. How often were Bruce and I dropped into the bottom of an eight-foot fleece sack? They would throw the fleeces to someone on top of the fleece platform and then they would drop the fleece down into the sack. The two in the bottom of the sack could climb to one side and turn their face to the sack. Then fleeces could be thrown down behind them. You would turn around and get to work. Now, this is where things could get nasty. If the person, generally an older sibling or cousin, had any kind of vengeance for you, they would intentionally throw the fleece on top of your heads. With suffocating anger, you would rip it off and start stomping. We had to work the fleece down the side of the sack and start stomping it down in all the loose areas. There was no revenge until you had worked your way out of the sack. No surprise that I am now allergic to wool and claustrophobic, but we laugh and retell this story over and over.

Branding is a spring event that takes the entire clan to accomplish. The different ranchers choose their day to brand and then the whole community shows up to help. It starts early in the morning with the women in the kitchen preparing an enormous meal for 60 or 70 people. The men, and kids lucky enough to have a horse that day, head out to gather in the cattle. Always there are cattle to be sorted, old cows that lost their calf, yearlings that will be butchered or bulls that you want to pull away from the heard. You gather the cattle, ideally in a corner of a fence and then the owner of the cows works his horse into the 300 head of cattle, spots the cow to be removed and then his horse works the cow out to the edge of the herd. Those of us holding the outer edge of cattle must be on the alert, follow the cow with our eye and be ready to maneuver the cow away from the herd. While this is taking place, the older men are readying the branding fire and getting the branding irons red hot. The cowboys continue to hold the cows and calves in the corner and the ropers start to work into the herd and catch the calves by their heels, they drag them out of the herd where two people throw the calf down. One sits on the ground at the back of the calf, a foot is placed firmly on the calf's butt and you hold the upper leg out straight. The other person puts a knee on the calf's neck and bends the front leg and holds on tight. The calves are vaccinated, ear marked, branded and castrated. You give your partner a nod and both jump up off the calf and away he goes. I have held hundreds of calves and never tire of the feeling of being a part of a job that takes all of us to accomplish the task. One by one for hours the banding continues until the last calf is roped. Tired, dirty, laughing we all head to the house to enjoy a roast beef, mashed potatoes, gravy, home-made rolls, salads and pies. Reward enough for a job well done. April is filled with brandings, and still after 94 years each one is filled with anticipation.

I do not want to forget about Thanksgiving. This is the one holiday that my mother's family came to our ranch to celebrate. The Robert and Ethel Philps family lived 60 miles away in Challis, Idaho. My grandfather was a dentist and came to the Challis area in 1901. He traveled to all the mines in the area taking care of the miner's dental needs. He met my grandmother in church, she was the daughter of a mining engineer that worked in Custer, Idaho. Years later, my grandfather bought my grandmother a cattle ranch and she ran the ranch until she was 95 years old. Another hard working, moral, loving, set of aunts and uncles to further establish my firm family foundation. They would arrive at our ranch with good cheer, filling our home with laughter, singing, and tall tales. More cousins by the dozens for me to play with until dusk---happy, happy memories.

My Dad, Harold Hancy McFarland was born December 1, 1913, in Poplar, Idaho. Dad was not just my Dad; he was my friend and my hero. We laughed and played together. Actually, we rough housed a lot, it drove my Mom crazy. He would pinch me and I would tear after him to pinch him back. Sometimes this led us tearing out of the house screaming that I would catch him, he was a really fast runner and I don't think I ever did catch him. We would end up down at the barn and turn to our joint passion, horses. Sunday night we would all settle into our tiny den and listen to Gun Smoke on the radio or crawl up into Dad's lap and he would read us the funny papers. He made all kinds of work on the ranch fun. On our way out to feed the cows in the winter, he would take the time to hook up our sleds so we could hooky-bob. He could turn a day of getting firewood into a picnic and baseball game. After working hard in the hay fields, he would be the one to initiate a game of No Bears Out Tonight. We would all go out in the dark of the night and then he would be the bear to seek us all out. Terrifying as a young girl, but so much fun.

First thing every morning dad would go to the foot of the stairs and call, "Suz, rise and shine." In fifteen minutes, you were expected to be at the barn, in good spirits, to milk your cow. Ranch life is hard work, it takes the entire family to get the job done. Thanks to Dad that hard work is a precious memory.

Dance. Could my dad dance, he had rhythm placed deep within his soul. He could waltz, two-step, polka and tap dance. When those long legs heard music, they started gliding across the floor. We danced at home often. As a little girl Daddy would have me step on the toes of his boots and we would dance up a storm. One of my favorite memories is watching my Dad and Mom dance. Dad would swirl her around the floor and both would have enormous grins on their faces. In those days there were dances most every weekend that the entire family attended. As a little girl I would dance until I was exhausted and then curl up in my parent's coat and wake up the next morning in my bed. My dad's happy spirit was evidenced in his singing and whistling. Driving a tractor farming you could hear dad singing, "KKKatie bbbeautiful KKKKatie, you're the ooonly ggggirl that I adore." Horseback you would hear him coming in out of the fields from irrigating, whistling a happy tune.

Dad was a tall, good looking cowboy. He had brown wavy hair, he brushed it straight back and it fell into perfect waves. Dad had large calloused hands, hands that were hard working but hands that were so gentle and full of love. Dad implanted in me a love for nature and especially animals. He grazed our cattle on the open range and we spent countless hours together horseback moving cattle to better feed. I remember overhearing him tell someone that came to visit, "My daughter Sue, can ride any horse on this ranch." That filled my heart with so much love. I was so happy to hear of his pride. When we would return to camp from a long day's ride, tired and hungry Dad would gently remind me to care for my horse before myself. He taught me how to work and how to play. He instilled in me the importance of forgiveness and living in order with God. He gave me the desire to have good morals by his example. Often, I have tried to remember how Dad disciplined me. I held him in such high respect, all he had to do was raise his eye brows or give me a sad look and I instantly knew I was doing something that displeased him. I was disciplined by his gentle guidance and my longing to please him. His most significant lesson to me was about Spirit. Dad was a deep sensitive person, a thinker and a person of great wisdom. His faith and reverence in God allowed him to have great understanding, good council and a sensitivity to the spirits of others. When I would have a problem or a concern, Dad would listen to me well, and would tell me to listen to my heart. Now, I know that Dad had allowed the inner core of himself to have communication with his God and he kept that active and alive by his quiet interchange with God. This had nothing to do with religion, his was the outcome of a man who believed he was made in the same image as God and if he spent quiet time with his maker, he would receive direction and knowledge.

As a boy my father was responsible at a very young age to tend his father's sheep. At the age of 12 he was spending his summers alone in the mountain above our ranch caring for a band of sheep. A band of sheep consists of 1,000-1,500 sheep. He was a Sheppard. He had a horse; a camp site and he daily moved his sheep form area to area for good feed. He was responsible to keep predators out of the band and to maintain the sheep's health. His father would come every couple of weeks to bring him new supplies, to give him the latest family news, advice, and encouragement. I like to think that this experience was fundamental in my dad becoming such an incredible father. He was the protector of his flock. Can't you imagine he had plenty of time to ponder, to grow and become assured of himself. His aloneness gave him the opportunity to connect with his maker and form a tight bond.

I was married and living in Northern Idaho when I got the phone call from my Mom that my Dad was very ill. Life, one soon finds out is a mixture of pleasures and great sadness. That is really what this story is all about, being able to look at your sadness, feel, really feel your sadness, but then turn sorrow into joy and keep going on with your life. Really, we only have two choices when we encounter great sadness. We can give into it and become a miserable bitter person or we can confront it, analyze it, put it in perspective and use the experience as a stepping stone for new growth in our lives. I surely did not have this maturity at the age of 22 when confronted with my father's impending death.

Jim and I met my mother in Salt Lake City where dad was to have brain surgery. To this point in my life I had never faced separation let lone, death. I had the privilege of having a Mom and Dad who were devoted to each other and to their children. I felt privileged growing up. It had nothing to do with having money or position because we didn't. I always knew I was loved; I always knew my folks expected my best and I always knew their solid base and example would ground me.

My Dad had brain cancer. This was my first true test of faith and reliance on Jesus. Jim and I made frequent trips to Carmen to see my dad after his surgery. We drove in late one night, I was desperate to see my Dad. Mom and Dad were in bed, I knocked softly on their bedroom door and said, "I'm home Daddy." He rolled over and said, "Oh Suz, your home!" Those where Dad's last words to me. That night he fell into a coma and a few weeks later went to be with his

Lord.

Momma, Mom but never Ma. Ethel Fern Philps was born, April, 13, 1914, to Robert and Ethel Philps of Challis, Idaho. Mom was born with a good-sized birthmark on her left check. She was born and raised on a cattle ranch beneath the red, orange bluffs of the Salmon River. This family run ranch was like most ranches, it took the entire family to accomplish the work that had to be done. Grandma and her five children plus a good hired man or two accomplished the task. They held the ranch together during the depression and during World War II. Mom learned her ranch management skills form her mother. Grandma was in charge of the ranch, she hired and fired the crew, set the work schedule and told how and when things would happen. She raised chickens, turkey and a huge garden. She cooked three enormous meals a day and never had less than a dozen people around her table. Perhaps this example is what made Mom, an excellent ranch wife, she was a take-charge kind of woman. Mom was the only one of her siblings to go to college and obtain a degree.

This degree is what brought her to Carmen, Idaho. She was hired to teach school at Lower Carmen. She lived in with a family and rode a horse to the school each morning. She built the fires and hauled the water and had the lessons ready when her students arrived. This county school could have 30 or 40 students ranged in ages from 6 to 14. Mom was the only teacher. The school was also used as a dance hall and most every weekend the community of ranchers gathered to dance and socialize. Shy Harold McFarland meets, not shy at all, Ethel Philps, they fell in love on the dance floor. They were both 27 years old when they married.   When their second child was due Mom retired from teaching but would return to it after her family was raised. Dad built Mom a log cabin on the ranch, it was small, no indoor plumbing and a bed that let down out of the wall. The original cabin was added onto until eventually the house was shaped like a Z. A comfortable home where they raised their 5 children.

When you think of the word "housewife," the image comes to mind of this lady that virtually has nothing to do, like in <u>Father knows Best</u>. A ranch housewife has endless work in front of them. There is the house, the children, cooking. Plus raising hundreds of chickens, making butter, raising a huge garden, tending the yard and helping on the ranch whenever the need arises. She cooked huge meals for shearing, branding, bull sales, and Grange dinners. In her spare time, she raised beautiful roses, practices the piano and read.

Mom was the community fun organizer. She set up bands for dances, hosted dinner parties, card parties and made sure everyone had a special birthday. She entertained church groups, school faculty and endless ranch family friends. Sundays would find her getting out her fine china for guests invited for dinner. Most weekends Mom and Dad had a date to dance or socialize with friends. Mom could come in from hard work in the barn, filthy dirty and tired. Bath, do her hair, put on her make-up and dress elegantly, and be out the door with a smile on her face.

When I was in high school, I came home complaining about my Spanish teacher. The next thing I knew, Mom had Spanish lessons on tape and was practicing her long-forgotten Spanish, as she did her housework. The next year she applied and got the Spanish teaching job. Great, now I had my mother for a teacher, not so cool in high school. At this point, Mom started having foreign exchange students living with us. We had girls and boys from all over the world. They would go to school and help Mom and then be a part of our family. Mom hosted international nights at the high school and with the money she earned took her advanced Spanish students to Mexico, year after year. Mom retired from teaching to take care of Dad in his illness. After losing the love of her life she was restless and decided to travel.

She made contact with many of the foreign exchange students that had lived with us and she took off on a world tour staying with her former students all throughout Mexico, South America, England, and France. Oh, I forgot to tell you that after she conquered Spanish, she also learned

French and some German.

Returning from her travel she was never quite able to fill her time with purpose as she had done all her life. Mom always fought depression, from a very young age until the very end. Depression is endless in its pursuit; it strikes when you least expect it. Her depression was always so baffling to me because I admired her many fine qualities and accomplishments and I thought she was beautiful. After my dad's death she struggled desperately trying to find a balance to stabilize herself. Several years later we found out she had cancer. After a considerable battle, she was lying on her death bed. I said to her "Mom do you want to go home." Meaning, "heaven," so she could be with Daddy. She looked at me with fear and shook her head "no." She mistook me, thinking I was asking her if she wanted to go to Carmen. I said, "No, do you want so go to heaven and be with Daddy." She turned her head to me and smiled. She died hours later.

Could that little girl with the birthmark on her check have suffered feelings of ugliness, unworthiness, isolation? Did she spend a lifetime, desperately, trying to fill the empty places in her heart?

Grandma
By Tom Smith

Stars above my grandma,
Make sounds like foreign languages.
Smell like new washed hair
And feel like baby lamb's wool.
They taste like cherry bubblegum
And move like the stormy weather wind
But they look like shimmering gold, newly polished
Right out of the mine.

Chapter 2

The Carmen Creek Kids

Train up a child in the way he should go,
And when he is old, he will not depart from it.
Proverbs 22:6

Kathy "Sue" Smith, born April 21, 1949, the fourth child to Harold and Ethel McFarland. I was born in Salmon, Idaho in a birthing home and within a week brought home to Carmen Creek. The story goes, Mom was busy baking pies for branding when it became apparent that someone else was going to have to take over the job. My name Kathy was given to me by my Uncle Glen. In the news, right before I was born, was a story about a little girl that had fallen down a water well. It seems it took several days to recover her, thankfully she was still alive. This little girl's name was Kathy.

There was a totally different perspective of raising children in my generation. We were wanted, we were loved, but by no means were we coddled. Our needs were met, but a great deal of the first few years of life were with whomever had a little extra time. From the time I could toddle I spent every spare minute with my Grandma Gudrun. She lived in a large two-story house. It seemed grand to me but looking back I am sure it was hard to heat in the winter and unbearable hot in the summer. She had the gentlest soul. She was always busy but took the time to let me be a part of her tasks. She asked me questions and listened so well, I felt important and needed. I don't think Grandma Gudrun was ever very happy on Carmen Creek. She was raised in the open plains and our mountains frightened her. We would be at coffee time and she would say to her sons, "Well, tomorrow I would like to move to Arche's." The next day her boys would show up with a flatbed trailer and move her belongings to a small bunk house on Uncle Arche's ranch. She once lived in the upstairs of our house, and a bunk house by her big house. I remember one time when I was staying with her down at Uncle Arches. I went out to the outhouse and got locked in. I don't know how long I was in there but when she found me, she felt so bad. After that, each time I went to the outhouse she always walked out with me. She was living in the bunkhouse up by her big house when I was 5 years old. July 24, 1954 the family was going to take a break from the hay field, spending the day at Salmon Hot Spring. This was a rare treat and I was so excited. We drove up to pick up Grandma and Dad sent me in to get her. She was sitting in a cushioned rocking chair sleeping. I touched her on her arm to wake her and she did not respond, I tried several times. I got frightened and ran to my Dad and told him Grandma was sleeping and I could not wake her up. She was

taken back to the flat land to be buried with her
family.

> *When God's weeding in life's garden,*
> *Where the noxious weeds can grow.*
> *Will you be a plant,*
> *That He leaves to grow?*
> *Grandma Gudrun*

My Uncle Glen married my Aunt Norma
when I was about 5 years old. She was a city girl
form New York City. She was a registered nurse
and had come to Salmon to work in their new
hospital. Aunt Norma was crazy fun, everyday
spent with Aunt Norma was a day to remember.
We dressed up in old costumes, did art projects,
sang, and laughed hilariously. She was there to
help with the pain of losing my Grandma. She was
there, way into my adult life, she always listened,
never ridiculed, always encouraged.

Dave, Bruce and Lee my oldest and dearest
friends. Carmen Creek cousins. When I think back
on our childhood, I realize we lived in a time and a
place where children were allowed to be children.
We were raised to be responsible but we were
given almost limitless freedom. Our ranch was at
the top of the valley. Dave and Bruce's ranch was
next and Lee's ranch down the creek further. One
day when I was 6 years old, I decided to catch my
horse and go see Dave and Bruce. I had been
given a dime, a very rare occurrence, and I wanted
to show it to them. I put the dime in my shirt

pocket and went to catch my horse. Now saddling a horse when you are short is not an easy adventure. It takes a determined rider and a very willing horse. I got the horse in the barn and fed it plenty of grain. I then put the saddle and blanket in the hay manger. I climbed up into the manger and threw the blanket over the horse's neck and then down to his back. I then tried the same procedure with the saddle. However, saddles are heavy and little girls not as strong as they like to think they are. Finally, with enough perseverance I got the saddle in approximately the right place. I got down out of the manger and tightened the cinch. I took off down the mile-long trail, through the creek bottom, that lead to Dave and Bruce's ranch. About half-way to their place my saddle slipped and went under my horse's belly and obviously I fell off. I was no worse for ware and it certainly wasn't the first time I had fallen off of a horse. I reached in my pocket to check on my dime and found it missing. I crawled all over looking for my dime but to no avail. I burst out in tears and sat there screaming for a good period of time. I finally got up, undid my cinch to let the saddle fall to the ground and then led my horse up to a big rock to re-saddle. I guess the moral to this story is self-reliance and a check in pride. Sixty some years later I still walk that trail and each time I get to the spot where I was dumped, I look for my dime.

It was about this period of my life when I truly believed I was Hopalong Cassidy. My exposure to Hopalong came from listening to his weekly adventure on the radio. He soon became my hero. Hopalong was bold and brave and could handle himself in every situation. I spent days on end being Hopalong. I rescued those in needs, I stood up for the underdog, and served justice to those I deemed guilty. For Christmas, Santa brought me a Hopalong Cassidy outfit. I had black chaps, a black hat, and greatest of all, pistols. Ivory handles on shiny silver, equipped to hold caps. The holster was black and decorated in silver. This cinched the deal, I was Hopalong. I rode the range and willed my power over all immorality.

So, the general rule was, you get up in the morning and do your chores. If the family didn't have some big work event going on the kids were pretty well kicked out of the house and not expected to return until chore time in the evening. Also, the men all worked together and wherever the men were, the kids were. What I'm getting at, my cousins and I were always together. This amount of freedom led to great adventures.

We spent endless days in the sagebrush hills that surrounded the ranches. To put this in perspective these hills covered hundreds of acres of land. Some days we were explorers because we often went places, we had never been. Perhaps we were looking for gold. Other times we would play cowboy and Indians. One time we hauled shovels out into the hills determined to find an Indian grave and dig it up. We had heard Indians were buried with all of their belongings; we were seeking treasures. By the time we had hiked a couple of hours we had scared ourselves to death talking about Indian spirits and their sacred burial grounds. We imagined sounds, perhaps even voices, we were spooked by a moving sage or the twitter of a bird. We knew how Indians talked to each other with bird sounds. With total fear in our faces we turned tail and ran all the way home.

Underlying all this adventure was some internal fear. We were born the late 1940's. We were of the baby boom generation. The United States used an atomic bomb on Hiroshima in 1945. This happening was still very much a part of adult conversation. I cannot say that I understood what an atomic bomb was, but I knew it was terrible and deadly. Add to this we were in the midst of the cold war with the Soviet Union. The nightly news and again the conversation at coffee time could turn very intense. This being said, those free-spirited cousins out in the hills for the day were turned into panic if a plane flew overhead. We would dive for the biggest sagebrush, convinced the Soviet's had come to get us and our world was coming to an end.

Our mode of transportation in these days were our stick horses. Stick horses in our day were just that, a stick picked up off the ground that became your horse for the day. We would not consider leaving the ranch without our stately steeds. We knew their color, breed and disposition. Some were tried and true, others you had to buck out each time you mounted. We proudly galloped through the hills to our destinations. My stick horse was always "Red." The first real horse I ever rode was Wings, an old red horse. Then we had a horse named, Red. Also, the first horse of my very own was red. Just plan red was fine for me. Many years later I found a very dear friend who shared these same feeling about red horses.

Plain Ol' Red
By Denise McRea

People praise a palomino for its coat of shining gold
Fancy patterns are a bonus where paints are bought and sold

Pretty colors sure do catch the eye, but something must be said
For foals that come into this world just wearing plain ol' red.

Plain ol' red wins at the races, plain ol' red's rode by the boss
Nothing in this world is worth more than that plain ol' red kid's hoss

Plain ol' reds have plenty heart, plain ol'
reds have plenty of speed
Them sorrels have the savvy that good cow
horses need

And a lot of old time cowboys chose plain
ol' reds for mounts
'Cuz they were looking at the inside, and
that's the part that counts.

One time the four of us decided to go
hiking out behind Lee's place, we were soldiers
marching off to war. We came to a large ditch and
we took off our shoes to wade across. The boys
quickly dried their feet, the best they could, and
put their shoes back on. I hardly ever wore shoes
from the end of May to the end of September but
had on a pair of little brown lace up shoes. After
crossing the ditch, I tied the laces together and
threw them over my neck. We march on to
conquer the world and played all day long crossing
several more ditches. At the end of the day when
the sun started to set behind the hills, we knew
we had better high-tail it home. We arrived at
Aunt Mary's hot, tired and hungry and me without
any shoes! So, you must understand, in those
days' kids had one pair of shoes. On my two mile
walk home I was faced with how I was going to tell
my Mom I had lost my shoes. The news was not
well received and I was lectured about

responsibility and the value of a dollar. The next spring my Uncle Frank found my shoes in one of his irrigation headgates.

Another time Dave and Bruce and I decided to go camping, we were probably about 8 and 9. We spent some time figuring out what we would need. And got things packed up. Now, in those days sleeping bags came in one size "large." They were made of canvas and lined with flannel. We decided we would get by with one. We rolled the thing up and could hardly lift it. We decided if we ran a pole through it then two of us could carry it. The third person had a frying pan, potatoes and hamburger and matches. We took off down over the hill from David's house heading to new country. We wanted to explore the hills above the Cutler ranch. We had heard tell there was a lake up there somewhere. Often, we had to stop and rest and trade places, the carrying pole, in hindsight, much bigger than necessary, made our shoulder burn like fire. The hill was steep and we truly had no idea where this so called "lake" was located. I don't know if it was persistence, resolve or willpower but we continued climbing until it started to get dark. At this time, we had just creased a ridge and decided we had better make camp. We assured ourselves that explorers make dry camps all the time. We got the sleeping bag rolled out and a fire built. In our planning we had forgotten a few important things, salt and butter to fry the spuds in. Thankfully, by now it was near dark because we were not able to see our raw hamburgers and burnt potatoes. Three kids in a sleeping bag on a step mountain ridge---- In the morning we were down the hill a good distance, but as I recall we all had a great night's sleep. Years later I would go out into those hills horseback searching for that lake. Finally, one day I found a tiny little spring that filled a pond not much bigger than your bathtub. I guess in the high mountain desert, even that is called a lake.

I don't remember getting in trouble very often. In hind sight I have often wondered, was that because our parents were unaware of our antics, or they were just broad minded enough to think we would learn by our mistakes. I have to believe that we were not half as sneaky as we thought we were.

Here is an example of Carmen Creek kid trouble. Dave and Bruce and I had heard, or dreamed up that the way to check a pig's health is to straighten out their tails and if they curl right back up, they are healthy. However, if you straighten them and they stay straight they are ill. We enter the pig pen and start chasing several litters of weanling through the mire to achieve our goal. We slip, we slide and when we accomplish our goal we scream and yell, "Check this pig out!" We would watch to determine the fate of the squealer. Was he a keeper? Now pigs make a remarkable amount of noise when being chased, let alone, when they get their tails pulled. Don't you think every father would appreciate our willingness to chase the entire herd of pigs around pulling their tails, to determine their well-being. "Not true," Uncle Arch came out of the house trying to scream over the top of all of the combined noise of kids and pigs. By the time he reached the pig pen he was not a happy camper. He bopped all three of us out of that pen and yelled at the top of his voice. We quickly became firm believers that our efforts had not been valued. I have pondered this situation for years. Why was Uncle Arch so upset? It couldn't have been because we were beyond filthy, we may not have rolled in pig crap every day but we were never concerned about cleanliness. Were we devaluating the weaner pigs, market value, by running their fat off? Were there sows in that pen that could have potentially hurt us? Sixty years later and I still am unaware of my crime.

The only other time I remember him getting mad at us was when we were in the mountains cutting poles. Dad and Arch could cut a 50-foot-tall poles down in four or five whacks. Well, there was an extra ax and so Dave, Bruce and I were taking turns trying to cut down our own tree. This tree was no more than 3 or 4 inches in diameter. We hacked and hacked at this tree for better than an hour. Finally, we were so excited when it started to fall. We jump up and down and yell, "TIMBER." The only problem was the tree's trajectory was right in line with Uncle Arch. When that lodge pole pine hit him across the back, he went down like he had been shot. We thought we had killed him! We stood motionless stunned, until 30 seconds later when Uncle Arch jumped to his feet. We took off running, not a real good idea.

Smoking cigarettes in the 1950's was viewed much differently than today. There was no research teaching of the hazards of smoking. It was a common social practice enjoyed by most, certainly by all the cowboys in my life. I am just trying to prepare you, sin, in this story was our stealing not our smoking. Roll your own cigarettes were what real cowboys smoked. Every man carried a packet of thin, 2 1/2- and 3-inch papers, held together by a cardboard scarf around them. The tobacco came in small muslin sacks with a yellow pull string on the top. To assemble a cigarette, you dumped a small amount of tobacco on the thin paper and then rolled it up. You lick the long edge of the paper to seal the cigarette together. Then you twisted the ends so the tobacco does not fall out. You light a match off the seat of your pants and light your cigarette. I've seen it done a million times. Call it adventure, call it daring, call it stupid, but the challenge was to wait until the men were out in the fields and the women were giving a card party or whatever else would keep them occupied. We would sneak into a bunkhouse, we all had hired men, and we would steal cigarette papers and tobacco. Off we would go for the creek bottom to our latest hideout to have a smoke. So, come to find out, watching a cigarette being rolled and doing it, are entirely two different things. There are a few important things you learn. One, lighting a match off the seat of your pants is a skill that must be acquired, practice does not always make perfect. Two, if you do not use enough tobacco, the paper burns very quickly and you will soon find yourself without eyebrows. Three, if you use too much tobacco the burn down your throat is intense, you head to the creek and bury your head in the water, thinking surly you are going to die. Thankfully, trial and error never increased my skills. To add sin to sin, we surely did not want our folks to know that we had been smoking so we would creep back to the house, sneak in and steal a box of Jello or Kool-Aid to eat to cover the smell of cigarette. Somehow, we failed to figure, they would notice our blue or orange tongues.

One day when we had successfully made it to our hide-out with our confiscated cigarette paraphernalia, we were just starting the process of rolling when we were attacked by our older cousins and they stole all our goods.

There were days when we could find papers but no tobacco. No problem, we had good imaginations. We knew that the Indians smoked and they did not have tobacco. Safe to say we had no idea what a tobacco plant looked like. We started searching around and discovered a weed the red, brown color of tobacco. This plant grew in our less productive fields, it is about 12 to 16 inches tall. In the fall they have an incredible amount of dried up seed pods on them. We always had access to empty tobacco sacks and we started filling them full of our new-found secret. Bingo- perfect for roll your own's. Well, almost perfect, this stuff burned fast, you were lucky to get two puffs before the cigarette was gone. Also, the taste was near dreadful, only us hard nail smokers were man enough to continue to try to acquire a desire for this particular taste. Recently, I asked Dave if he knew the name of the weed we smoked, his reply was instant, "Tobacco Weed." A plant specialist identified this weed for me, Dock Weed. Thank God they were not poisonous.

We all had guns and learned to shoot at an early age. We had an overpopulation of ground squirrels on the ranches and we were encouraged to shoot as many as possible. It was a great way to improve your fast draw but after a while it lacked thrill. Again, imaginations running wild we decide we could kill a tremendous amount of jack-rabbits if we went out at night in the old willy's jeep and spot lighted them. We would head up to the west side of the Parmenter place where the rabbits were more prolific. So, remember none of us are over 12 or 14 years old, no problem we all learned to drive in the hay-field when we were 6 or 7 years old. I want you to picture where we are going. There is a steep dugway road that leads up to these fields. The fields are really just the rounded off tops of the foot hills. It is dark, the fields are not that large with steep edges off the fields in every direction, and probably we were not as good at driving as we thought we were. We took turns, someone had to drive, the rest of us stood up in the back of the jeep with our 22 rifles. The driver would take off after a rabbit in hot pursuit and the shooters were trying to stand up, aim their guns and kill the rabbit. Shrieks of laughter, grabbing each other to help balance, and victory cries when a rabbit was nailed. Hour after hour we would trade positions and continue to massacre the grass eating nuisances off our croplands.

Though it sounds like we were a bunch of wild orangutans we did have a great deal of responsibility. Our cattle range was in the National Forest and covered thousands of acres. We would leave the ranch horseback trailing hundreds of cows. We would take them down Carmen 6 miles and hit the highway where we could cross the cows and calves across a large steel bridge over the Salmon, River. We then headed them north into the BLM sagebrush hills and continue to parallel the river until we got to Bird Creek. We would head them up this steep, narrow, roadless, canyon until it got dark, 12 hours in the saddle. Camp consisted of whatever food fit rolled up in your coat, we did not have anything as elegant as saddle bags, your saddle for your pillow and your wet saddle blanket for your blanket. This cattle drive takes place in early May. The days may be warm but when the sun goes down in Lemhi, County it gets cold. We all scavenged a huge pile of firewood. Pulling our saddles as close to the fire as possible to start the night of endless turning, back to the fire, front to the fire. No fire, rebuild fire, back to the fire, front to the fire. Up before the sun, saddle up and keep trailing cows up the canyon. If all goes well, we will come out on the saddle of the divide, head north on Napoleon ridge and be to camp by sundown. One of the men have come up the Stormy Peak road and set up a wall tent, a fire is a welcome sight and the smell of a steaming stew help us push the cattle to the end of today's journey. I can tell you that these rough accommodations look like a palace after sleeping out in the open on the cold rocky ground.

One year when we were older a bunch of us cousins were sent on this ride without the help of any adults. If you have never been responsible to push hundreds of cows up steep trails where they do not want to go, you cannot imagine how much work it is. Your horse is tired, you are tired but the only way to end the misery is to accomplish the task. We spent the long cold night sleeping out as we did every year. We got up to snow on the ground and it steadily snowed all day long. Cows do not like to travel in the snow. They like to hold up with their backs to the wind. This just was not an option. We had coats, and cowboy hats but no gloves or scarves, no chaps or raincoats. We knew we had at least a 12-hour day before we toped the hill. Our survival depended on getting this herd up the hill. Though we had heard our share of swear words growing up on the ranch, we were forbidden from using them. This particular day gave us the opportunity to use every word we had ever heard many times over. By the time we crested the hill, we were near froze to death. We turned the cows and headed to our long dreamed of wall tent, warmth and hot food. When we got to the designated camp, no one was there. We were soaked to the skin, snow still falling and now inches deep. We were just starting to realize the danger we were in if help didn't come. We started piling brush and made a huge fire, we had no food left, it started to get dark. Off in the distance we thought we heard a motor. We were desperate for one of our fathers to show up and take over the responsibility of making decisions. Finally, the truck shows up and out step one of our cousins, same age as us! Now, to be honest he had also had a miserable day. The road had been slick all the way up the switch backs and by the time he hit the divide he was pushing snow with the bumper. After hearing his story, we all piled in to get camp set up. Wall tents are a two-man job but a 4 or 5 kid job. You have to run a large pole down the length of the tent and then set each end of the pole up on cross bars. The trick is holding it all up while people work on opposing sides to anchor the tent down. Tent in place we unrolled sleeping bags, while others started in on supper. After getting our stomachs full of hot food, and getting dried out a bit, things did not look so bad. The next morning, we woke up to 6 inches of snow, but it had stopped snowing. We ate a hardy breakfast of bacon, eggs, and pancakes, saddled our horses and started our 20-mile ride home.

This is how the cattle got to range in the spring. It was then our job to move the cows to higher and higher pastures as the grass developed. We had a cow camp on Moose Creek and many summers our fathers hired a rider to do the majority of this riding. Some of us kids were designated the riders "helper," and stayed in the mountains weeks at a time helping move cattle daily. One-time Dave, Bruce and I were living with the rider when we discovered not far from our camp was an old miner living in Melhouse Meadow. There were still old miners living throughout the mountains but this one held our attention because he did his mining in the nude.

Our camp was located near a huge eroded, wash that had been caused by a miming dispute. Miners had built a dam to block off Moose creek for their miming purposes. In the night someone blew up the dam and caused a large amount of water to go down Dump Creek, a draw that typically housed just a small trickle of water. An enormous gorge was developed. We found as we worked our way down this gorge and then climbed the steep bank, we could get glimpses of the naked miner.

Neal Allen was a miner and trapper that had a cabin not far from our camp. I was terrified of this man. He could walk into our camp without making a sound. At night sitting around the campfire he would just appear. He would settle himself in with a cup of coffee and start telling petrifying stories about a mountain lion that jumped him, or a bear that clawed his way into his cabin. On and on his stories went, he would finish his coffee and disappear into the dark. Bruce and I would creep into the miner shack we used for housing and climb into our bag; sure, we would not make it through the night.

Fall riding is everything in reverse, from May to September you spent day after day pushing the cattle higher and higher up into the mountains. Then about mid-September you start pushing everything down because you don't want cows to get snowed in. Fall rides have always been my favorite. The air is fresh and cold and the golden aspen against the green, green of the evergreens is breath taking. The idea is for individual cowboys to gather cows to a central location. When a large group is gathered, cowboys will make a big push and head them down over the divide and towards the foothill. This process is repeated over and over until you feel you have collected the majority of the cows. One night we had a bunch of cows gathered but the men figured

we did not have enough daylight to get them to
the divide and push them to the other side. The
solution to the problem was to leave Bruce and I
with the cows all night long, to keep them from
taking off. Whining or complaining was never
tolerated so we looked at each other and decided
to make it, yet another adventure. We had no
tent, no sleeping bags, no saddle, no saddle
blanket. We did have our coats, matches and one
pack of Fig Newtons. We made it through the
night, and I think we did a fair job of keeping the
cows where they were supposed to be. But to this
day I have never eaten another Fig Newton.

Once the cows were all over the divide all
the ranchers gathered the cattle off the low
foothills, forded them across the Salmon River and
headed them to Carmen Creek. At each person's
ranch cattle were sorted and put into pastures.
When the snow starts to fly the cows are fed hay.
They calve in January through March, brand in
April and out to the mountains in May. The cycle
has repeated for 94 years.

Irrigating grain in the Spring was another
time when the kids were called into service. First
understand, we live in a mountain valley and there
is no such thing as level ground. Some fields are
less steep than others but all have definite
declines. Second, these fields take days and days
of work of soil preparation before the seed can be
planted. The thick sod has to be plowed, then
disked, every time you turn the soil over, you

unearth Gods new gift of rocks. Every kid on Carmen Creek has picked more than their share of rocks. Then the field must be harrowed, planted and marked. When the grain first starts to pop out of the ground it is time for the first irrigation.

Water runs in large ditches above the field. The water is dammed up to allow the water to flow in lateral ditches right above the corrugations, corrugations are tiny indentions that run the length of the field. The job is a matter of team work among sibling, there lies the rub! The dominate team member is at the top of the field and the serf is at the bottom of the field. The person at the top is responsible to make sure there is a trickle of water running down each corrugation. The serf is responsible to walk up and down the rows, multiple rows, over and over removing obstacles and ensuring that each tiny trickle makes it to the bottom of the field. This is the scenario, serf places her hoe in a corrugation and hollers, "I don't have water in the ditch." Top dog hollers back, "I have, go find the problem." After several days of this, sibling dynamics that were never great, are at a boiling point. Serfs only justice is when they can be top ditch man. An interesting note on lack of women's rights. Boys had irrigating boots, girls irrigated barefoot. On warm days it was no big deal, but those cold early mornings the injustice was felt.

From the 5th of July to the middle of September we hayed. I have pictures of the hay equipment we used in the 50's and 60's and comparing them to the equipment of today, evidence in why we were in the hay field for months. I still own one of the first tractors that was bought for the ranch, my grandchildren call it the "baby." There were endless chores for everyone in the hay field. Some of mine were running errands for my Dad. "Run to the shop and get me a ¾ inch socket." I run like the world depends on this socket, get to the shop and search, terrified of not fulfilling my responsibility. I run all the way back into the fields and panting hand my Dad the socket. "Thanks Suz, I got it fixed without it."

I turned bales of hay to help them dry, up and down the fields, sun pounding down and me, with my scratched up bare feet walking through the stubble.

Best job of all was when I was about 7 years old and old enough to drive the tractor and slip. A slip a made from heavy lumber nailed together to make a 6x10 foot flat surface. This slip is attached to the tractor with a piece of cable or chain. My job is to drive the tractor as close to the bales of hay as possible and the kid on the slip reaches out with a hay hook and drags the bail onto the slip and stacks it. As I recall the slip held about 20 bales. I would then drive to the hay stack and the kid on the back would unload the bales one at a time and place them on a hay elevator that took the bales up to the top of the stack were the stacker built the stack. Being the tractor driver gave me a certain amount of power. We often hired town boys to help in the hay field and of course I was not about to take any lip from them. I found several deviant ways to make their days miserable. They would yell, "Get closer to the bales." Instantly the distance increases. Town kid, "YOU'RE A TERRIBLE DRIVER," slam on the brakes and his whole load has to be restacked. It was probably not a coincidence that my next responsibility in the hay fields was to rake hay. I was on a tractor all day long, in a field far away from anyone else, left to be head honcho of myself.

Tonight Dave, Lee and I are celebrating our 70th birthday together with a big family bash. (2019) I cannot tell you how thankful I am that God has allowed us to share our lives together. Even though we have each had successful, full lives, Dave, a rancher, Lee, a business man and my 30 years in education; each time we all get together we are like those rough-neck little kids again. Elaborating on the stories of our youth, running free and wild on Carmen Creek.

Chapter 3

From Triumph to Failure
My School Years

*We exult in our tribulations, knowing that
tribulation brings about perseverance; and
perseverance, proven character; and proven
character, hope; and hope does not disappoint,
because the love of God has been poured out
within our hearts through the Holy Spirit who was
given to us.*
Romans 5: 3-5

I was so excited for my first day of school. I
had watched my older sisters and brother head
out the door to catch the bus and be whisked off
to another world. They always came home in good
spirts full of laughter and tall tales. I was ready, I
stepped on that old, yellow school bus and sat
with my cousins. We were all country bumpkins
and hardly spent any time in town. I don't think I
was the only one apprehensive, proof was our
loud clamor, to cover our anxiety. By the end of
the first nine weeks of school I felt my self-
confident person start to fade away. I was in total
confusion, I didn't fit, I had always been so good at
everything on the ranch and now I felt like I was
stuck in the mud and it was slowly pulling me
under. I had never been a sad child, but now I

would wake up crying and my pillow case would be wet. I started having terrible stomach aches that lasted for hours. I isolated myself, I would catch my horse and head to the hills, sobbing as I covered the miles, frantic to try to understand what was wrong with me. Each day I stepped into the school I felt sick to my stomach, it was like I had been placed in a foreign country and expected to understand. A dyslexic child starts to see themselves as abnormal or stupid, which is exactly what they are told, either openly by some teachers or by some siblings with their taunts and teasing. Indirectly, dyslexics are made to feel inferior by being placed with the dumb kids. I truly had no idea what was the matter with me. No matter how hard I tried to listen to my teacher, no matter how many hours I studied, I was unable to function in the academic setting. Twelve years is a very long time to suffer. I learned all kinds of coping mechanisms to try to survive, I wrote everything sloppy to try and hide my multiple spelling errors. My Dad would act out or make word plays with spelling words so I could remember the order of the letters, my Mom spent countless hours honing my reading skills. Patiently, using all four learning modalities with constant repetition she worked with me night after night. Even in high school, Mom would read me a paragraph and then have me, read the paragraph. On and on we would go through the chapter. I would then get up very early in the morning and read the chapter again. An assignment that was meant to take 30 minutes could easily take me 4 hours. Multiply this by 5 subjects and you get the picture of the impossibility.

To survive I relied heavily on a few things I was very good at. In school I joined the drama club. This is kind of funny because in truth I had been acting since I started school. I was constantly on stage, trying to be someone I was not. Acting allowed me a freedom of being a totally different person. I was able to place myself into a character and feel their very souls. Being successful gave me great satisfaction. As a senior I was elected the best actress in the state of Idaho. Ironically enough, this success was accompanied by a scholarship to the University of Idaho.

God also gave me the ability to sing. In school I sang in all the school performances and tried out for parts in musicals. Because of my acting experience singing in musicals was a magical time for me.

Then of course I had my horses. The touch, sound, smell and movement of a horse has always had a way of putting my anxious mind into perspective. My Dad had me ride competitively throughout my high school years. I love him so much, he knew how I was suffering, how hard I was trying, so he went to the extra time and expense to make this happen for me. He knew this would give me a place to shine.

My mother was a teacher at my high school. One day I overheard Mom and the high school counselor talking about me. He was very confused because he had just given me an intelligence test and I had scored very high. You cannot believe this music to my ears. Sue McFarland scored very HIGH on an intelligence test. He went on to say he didn't know if I should be sent to college, but she is very smart. How can this be, how can I be dumb and smart at the same time!

God sent me a lifeline, to help me overcome the stigma of my perceived failures because of my dyslexia. When I was a freshman in high school, Jim Smith and I were snare drummers in the high school band. We started hanging out together during lunch and soon realized we were both in need of a good friend. Jim had lost both of his parents, at an early age, in a car accident. He was being raised by a well-meaning grandmother, but with little love in the home. I had wonderful caring parents but my academic failures had left me shattered. Education was very important to my family and I knew I was letting my parents down. School was still a daily struggle for me but now I had someone I could confide my feeling to. Someone who listened, cared and encouraged me. Likewise, I had someone to nurture, help him believe in himself, and help him analyze his real potential.

Also, I want to note, my oldest friends, Dave, Bruce and Lee, never looked down on me. Even though they excelled academically, Dave even became a Presidential scholar, they always treated me as an equal. I am so blessed that they never lost sight of the, inside me. They valued me, they believed in me and my abilities and respected me as a whole person. This mutual respect and love is what has held us soundly together. Allowing us a lifetime to cheer each other's accomplishments and a constant stability in times of trouble.

My dyslexia caused me to have:
1.   Complications with reading
2.   Difficulty with spelling
3.   Letter and number reversals
4.   Omitting sounds in words and words in reading and writing
5.   Difficulty in reading aloud
6.   Strong oral comprehension/weak reading comprehension
7.   Letters on page appear to move, appear blurry or out of focus
8.   Inability to differentiate speech sounds

Perhaps, the most frustrating thing about dyslexia is that your performance varies from day to day. On some days, reading may come fairly easily. However, another day, you are barely able to write your own name. This inconsistency is extremely confusing not only to the dyslexic person, but to others.

Myth: Smart people cannot be dyslexic or have learning disabilities
Fact: Dyslexia and intelligence are not connected.

Many dyslexia individuals are very bright and creative and have accomplished amazing things as adults.

What is dyslexia? Dyslexia is a general term for disorders that involve difficulty in learning to read or interpret words, letters, and other symbols, but that do not affect general intelligence. Dyslexia is neurological in origin, meaning that the problem is located physically in the brain. Dyslexia is not caused by poverty, developmental delay, speech, or hearing impairment. Snow, Burnes, and Griffin 1998.

According to multiple studies there are real structure differences in the brain. The brain is made up of gray matter and white matter. Gray matter is mostly composed of nerve cells and its primary function is to process information. White matter is found in the deeper part of the brain and acts as the connective fibers that create communication between the nerves. The white matter is also responsible for information transfer around the brain. Researchers Booth and Burman found that people with dyslexia have less gray matter in the left part of the brain than nondyslexic people. This could cause the problems with the sound structure of language. Also, it has been indicated dyslexics also have less white matter. This combination of less grey matter in the language area in the brain and less white matter to transmit language is the heart of the dyslexic's problem. Laurie Cutting explains the disadvantage of less white matter. When you are reading you are essentially saying things out loud in your head. If you have decreased white matter integrity in this area, the front and back part of the brain are not talking to one another. This would affect reading because you need both to act as a cohesive unit.

Many dyslexic adults become effective readers. It is believed that with enough repetition new brain nerve pathways can be created. Thankfully, I am one of these dyslexics. I credit my success to God; He has always been my comfort and my guide. Also, to my parents and Jim, and their never-ending support. I am also thankful for the work ethic I learned from working on the ranch. If you are given a tough job to do, you persevere until it is accomplished.

Research in dyslexia and success has found that each successful dyslexic, has a chip on their shoulder, to prove everyone who ever doubted their ability wrong, to prove that they are not stupid or thick. They are driven by their school failure and humiliation to do well in life. I was over 20 years old before I could read well, now a day

does not go by, without my reading for meaning
and for pleasure.

Chapter 4

Jim Smith

Soulmate
I spent days waiting for you,
Searching the crowds for your face.
I stopped breathing the moment
You recognized me, as you captured
My soul with your gaze.
Christy Ann Martime

Jim lived on Main Street of our small rural town. His grandmother rented a boarding house and lent out rooms. The first time I ever saw Jim, though at the time I didn't know his name, he was sitting on his front porch playing cards. As we drove by, I wondered why this rather plump boy would be playing cards on a beautiful day. This image made me feel so sad. I guess I compared it to my cousins and I always on the go with big plans to fill each day. So, I started watching for that boy each time the bus passed his house. Most often it was him leaving his house on his way to school. The next school year I again was staring out the bus window but never saw the fat boy of my interest. In his place was a tall, dark, very thin boy. This was my first year in high school and when I slipped into the band room this tall, very good-looking boy was standing up in the drum section. I too am a drummer and shyly took my place. Hence, Jim Smith walked into my life. The cute, fat boy had thyroid surgery and turned into my handsome knight.

Our friendship developed throughout high school. He is a year older and headed to the University of Idaho and left me to finish my senior year. Absence makes the heart grow stronger happened to be true in our case. We had developed a sound foundation of true friendship in high school but those letters that flew back and forth helped us to carve out a lasting love.

Jim is a Christian man; his personal strong faith is evident daily in his life. He has spent a lifetime serving others. One time we were in Spokane walking down the street when he turns to me and says, "Excuse me, I will be right back." He runs across the street to help a little old woman, safely across a busy road. Another time he was taking a class about serving special needs children. He had spent the afternoon in the classroom. When I saw him, the front of his shirt was all wet. He expressed what a wonderful afternoon he had spent with a down syndrome little boy, who had drooled all over him. A gentleman, walking on the outside of the sidewalk, opening doors, and pulling your chair out for you. How could I not fall for this gallant lad?

A soulmate is a person you have an immediate connection the moment you meet, a connection so strong that you are drawn to them in a way you have never experienced before. As this connection develops over time, you experience a love so deep, strong and complex, that you begin to doubt that you have truly loved anyone prior. Your soulmate understands and connects with you in every way and on every level, which brings a sense of peace, calmness and happiness when you are around them. And when you are not around them, you are all that much more aware of the harshness of life, and how bonding with another person is the most significant and satisfying thing you will experience in a lifetime. You are also all that much more aware of the beauty in life, because you have been given a great gift and will always be thankful. @relationshipgoals.

Last night Jim and I celebrated our 50th wedding anniversary with our family and friends (2018). Our love is a passionate love, we light each other's worlds. We are a perfectly matched team, each pulling our own share of the load.

My heart is having a hard time comprehending all the gifts that God has placed in our lives in order to reach this accomplishment. Jim and I both gave our lives to the Lord at very young ages. We met in high school and shared five precious years of friendship before we stepped into the responsibility of marriage.

Marriage is hard work, it is more giving and less taking, it is always being sensitive to your partner's needs. It is setting goals together and always working as a team. It is the absolute

knowledge that your partner will love you and lift
you up. None of this is a possibility unless you have
the common core of Jesus, the author of peace and
love.

Mountain top days, like this celebration are
wonderful. They help us express and remember
our blessings, share laughs and memories with our
loved ones. Valley days are where life takes place.
How we respond, how we act, how we encounter
losses. Moving through the valley in constant
communication with the Light for daily direction.
Hard work—one day at a time. Our best days are
ordinary valley days. Days where we wake
together, have a purpose to accomplish, a pleasant
evening where we share the day's events, then
cuddle up for a good night's rest.

God has blessed us with great joys and with
enormous grief. In truth it is the sorrow that
secured our clutch on Jesus—knowing there is no
way through without his strength. The Holy Spirit
guides one breath at a time, a step, a day, showing
the way.

Devine love is not luck, it is a choice. A
decision that nothing in our being is enough to
engineer a productive, purposeful life on our own.
Your will has to make a choice...Go it on your own,
or go it under the guidance of the Holy Spirit. Jim
and I chose Jesus.

Thank you, Lord, for your daily guidance,
and your Light that has directed our way. Your gift
has allowed us to successfully complete 50 years of

marriage.

Chapter 5

Jim and Sue

Never Jim, never Sue,
Always Jim and Sue.
Lois Snook

Jim left for college in 1966, he headed to the University of Idaho. It was a long year for me, left in Salmon to finish my senior year. I missed Jim terribly but I was really busy, as always school took a consuming amount of time for me. Also, my brother was in college and so my Dad needed lots of help on the ranch. I saddled my horse the minute I got home from school and rode through all of the cattle. Anything that looked like they may calve that night I put into a coral. I also did the night lambing. I always loved the sheep, I also love being outside at night. Bringing ewes into the lambing shed, experiencing the new life and having the responsibility filled my heart with belonging. I guess I have always had the inner desire to help the helpless. My father sensed this in me at a young age. He would bring me the newborn calves and lambs that would have otherwise died because of cold or illness. I remember long nights spent nursing weak lambs and claves. I was able to sense their needs and willingly gave of myself to satisfy them. I would get up in the middle of the night to

warm a bottle of milk for a bum lamb or
motherless calf, and head off down to the barn by
myself. The nights were cold, but my warmth came
from the feeling in my heart; the satisfaction of
responding to the call coming from deep within my
being.

I was an emotional wreck in the fall of 1967.
My mother insisted that I was going to college, I
couldn't even imagine how I could possible turn
that into a success. The only bright spot was I was
going the University of Idaho and would be near
Jim. By the end of my first semester of college I had
passing grades but I was a disaster. I had ulcers,
had lost weight and was a nervous wreck. I knew I
needed an occupation and further education but I
was physically unable to continue college.
That Christmas Jim ask me to marry him. Of course,
the answer was "Yes." But I knew before we could
get married, I had to finish some kind of education.
My parents, Jim and I made the decision I would
move to Spokane, Washington and enter a
business college. Mom called an elderly uncle and
he knew of an apartment next to his house. It was
a tiny little apartment and I loved it. This was my
first experience of living in a city and it was
thrilling. My Uncle Jim O'Brian was bent over and
used a walker to get around. I had never met him
before but we bonded very quickly. He invited me
over for Sunday dinners. He made the best fried
chicken I have ever eaten. He would also take me
out on dates. He would dress up in a suit and

hobble out to his huge old car and away we go, bumping over curbs, to the cinema. Uncle Jim was amazingly self-sufficient. He had a rocking recliner chair in his living room that he sat in all the time. In order to get up out of the chair he would start rocking harder and harder. He would then throw his body out of the chair, grab his walker and take off. He had a big, beautiful house that he took care of. We had a wonderful year together. When I graduated and was ready to leave, he said to me, "Sue, thank you for listening to an old man's stories over and over again and always acting as if it was like the first time you had heard them." Several years later I heard he was in a nursing home and went to see him. I will never forget the big smile he gave me when I entered the room, he grabbed my hand and held it tight the entire time I was there. His attitude about life has inspired me.

This was one of the most beneficial academic years of my life. It was kind of like repeating high school, this repetition was exactly what I needed to fill in all the gaps from my academic shortfalls. This was my first time to feel good about myself in school. Living alone gave me an opportunity to grow up and know how to take care of myself. I walked to school each day, about two miles, to downtown Spokane. For holidays, I would ride the train to Missoula and Mom would pick me up and take me to the ranch.

Jim and I were married October 19, 1968 in a very beautiful Episcopal church in Moscow,

Idaho. Proof that it does not take a big fancy wedding to have a successful marriage; in attendance were my parents, and sibling, and Jim's Grandmother and his siblings. Also, a few of our college friends. Roger Swanson was Jim's best man and Linda McIntire was my maid of honor. After the wedding Dad took us all out to dinner. When we came home for Thanksgiving Mom had a reception at the Grange Hall, The Howard Cutler band played, and we all danced until late into the night.

I was still living in Spokane and didn't graduate until February 7, 1969. When I moved to Moscow Jim and I lived in an 8' x 30' pink Kit trailer. We lived in Lonies Trailer Park. The trailers were so close together you could hear your neighbors.

Sixty-nine was a heavy snow year. One night we had a blizzard and in the morning the snow was three feet deep and enormous drifts against anything solid. The wind had blown so hard, snow was packed up under our car in a solid ice block. Snow and cold, but Jim and I were blissfully happy, together forever.

I soon got a job in Moscow, working for Dr. Lee Sharp in the Department of Agriculture, right up my line. He was doing research on plant species; it was all very interesting. I traveled with him to south Idaho where he was doing field experiments. It was Dr. Sharp that encouraged me to start taking college classes again. I worked for him and took one or two classes a semester. I began to excel academically. It was a slow process mentally to overcome all the feeling of self-doubt and worthlessness but a small light was starting to shine.

That summer Jim and I moved back to Salmon. He had a job fighting wildfires for the Bureau of Land Management. We lived in an old bunk house on Uncle Arche's ranch that my Grandma used to live in. Wood cook stove, no running water and an outhouse, I was home and I loved every bit of it. I worked that summer helping my dad. I worked in the fields and helped him with the sheep and cattle.

My dad raised registered Morgan horses. I had been training horses for him since I was 12 years old. That summer he had a couple of young horses for me to get started. He always made me laugh. I would get a horse coming along good, ride into the barnyard and say "Dad, look what this little horse can do." Within a month he would have that one sold. I used to tease him, I had no idea what it would be like to ride a good seasoned horse, mine were always green. It was a lovely summer to relax in my favorite environment and bask in my family's love.

Jim and I found a box of old western novels in the bunk house. I had never read for pleasure; it was never pleasurable to read! We had no TV and saving every cent for our next year of school, so began reading. Jim would read a chapter out loud and the next day, when he was gone, I would read the next chapter. That night Jim would read the second chapter out loud. We did this through several books. Finally, with Jim's patience we would start taking turns reading paragraphs. It was a whole new experience for me. I was dying to know the next part of the story so it kept me motivated to keep stumbling along. I can't say fluency came that summer but a love for stories certainly did.

Before heading back to college and work that fall, I caught my horse and headed out on the west side to my secret place to have a little talk with God. I needed affirmation that I was following His pathway for my life. I reached the crest of the hill and followed an old game trial down to the hollow between three hills. On the small grassy level, I dismounted and lay on my back looking up into the deep blue sky. Lying there, I realized in Gods point of view, I was just one single, tiny, little spot on the earth, for a very short period of time. No matter how insignificant, I was His tiny dot and I knew with His help my life could have meaning. "Lord, please give me your guidance and direction?" I smell the sage and the dank odor of ripe grass and wait and wait. "I want you to love Me, and I want you to be the best wife you can be." After a period of time I rise, lift my hands to the Lord and say, "Yes Lord, I love you, and yes Lord, I will be the best wife I can be."

We headed back to college in 1969 for Jim's senior year. We were so excited because we had moved our tiny trailer out of town into a trailer park that had a yard and room to breathe. Also, to my complete delight, my oldest sister Kay and her husband Rob came back to school and lived in the same trailer park. We spent happy times that year. We could probably write a book on how to have fun when you are really poor! I continued my work at the college of agriculture and took classes. Jim was working in the campus creamery. So, between the old hens and mutton Mom sent us and milk, cheese and ice cream we ate pretty high on the hog.

As we entered campus that year there was a terrible unrest. The Vietnam War had been in progress since 1961 but things were really heating up and volunteer recruits were not enough to fill the quota needed. We got wind of a lottery that would take place December 1, 1969 to recruit more soldiers. The campus was split with anti-war protests on one side and ROTC (reserve officer training core) on the other. Every male on campus knew they could be the next to go to Vietnam. I was terrified that Jim would be chosen, we knew it was very likely and he was willing. I did not want to be left alone and so we made the decision to have a child.

We did not have a TV or a radio and so on that cold December evening we sat in our old Ford Falcon and listened to the numbers being drawn. They took 366 capsules and placed a day of the years in each one of them. They were drawn out one at a time and the birthday read. The first capsules chosen were the first men to go. The first capsule chosen was September 14, just five days after Jim's birthday. The tension notched up as we shivered in fear more than the cold. Number after number was drawn and then finally September 9th. He was number 263. We stumble back in the trailer really not knowing any more than we did before. Will he be called?

History tells us that 500,000 U.S. military personnel were serving in Vietnam in 1969. The first 195 birthdays that were choses in the lottery were called to service. "The cost and casualties of the growing war proved too much for the United States to bear, and the U.S. combat units were withdrawn by 1973." Britannica.

We had a double surprise that spring. I gave birth to a beautiful baby boy, Bryce Alan Smith was born in Gritman Memorial Hospital April 25, 1970 at 6:13 P.M. I was terrified of the whole birthing process, remember, I am the one that had pulled countless lambs and helped pull calves. I had watched the vet come out and do a C-section or replace a uterus from a prolapsed cow. I was fretting one day at a family gathering and my cousin Jack said, "You look like a pretty good replacement heifer to me," didn't appreciate that comment. I knew how things could go wrong. Jim kept telling me, in his quiet subtle way, "I think we should go to the hospital," I kept stalling, remembering tales of women in delivery for hours.

Finally, I consented, I got all settled in the room and Dr. Brooks comes in and checks me. He asked me if I wanted anything for pain. I said how long do you think it will be, and he said I think we will have a baby in 30 minutes. "No pain medicine I told him." Surely, I could stand most anything for 30 minutes. Ten minutes later we had our God given gift.

Jim finished his senior year and graduated with degrees in psychology and biology. He signed up for a master's program in counseling for the following year.

We returned to Carmen for the summer to once again live in the bunk house. However, this was a different story, we had a baby! He was a delight, and smothered in family attention. Bunk house living takes on a whole new life with a baby to care for. Constant wood chopping to keep the house the right temperature, hauling water to keep all clean and tidy, and washing diapers in the ditch and hanging them on the line. I was delighted to be a mother and Jim was a patient helpful father. Looking back on that summer I remember smiles, laughter, family parties, sewing with Aunt Katie and spending time with my Mom and Dad. This time it is so different, because now I was a mother.

Again, at the end of the summer I take my ride into the west side hills to have a little visit with my Lord, I pick a star filled night with a bright moon. I am filled with such blessed happiness, peace and contentment. An hour out I come to my quiet place and dismount from my horse. I lay on my back and look up at the stars, pondering my life's journey. I have it all, and yet I can feel there is still something out there, God has in mind for me to do. Lack of patience has always been my greatest obstacle. I have a mother and father that love me. I have a marvelous husband, and I am a mother. Little did I know that within this next year my tranquility would turn into one of life greatest tragedies? But that night the Lord spoke to me and said, "I want you to love me, I want you to be the best wife you can be, and I want you to be the best mother you can be.

I mount my horse, give it its head and tell him to take me home. He confidently heads out through the starry night, the motion of the horse beneath me gives me a feeling of confidence and reassurance. I love you Lord and I will listen to you, and gladly serve my husband and my child.

Our last year in Moscow. It was a busy year; I took classes and took care of Bryce. Jim had a heavy load of classes, took care of Bryce and worked nights at as a sawmill watchman. It was getting close to spring and Jim started sending out job applications. Jim graduated with his master's degree in counseling in 1971 and got a job as a counselor for the Coeur d'Alene Indians in Plummer, Idaho. I'll never forget the feeling of joy we shared when he came home from his interview. It was late when he pulled in and Bryce and I were already asleep. I heard him come in, he was doing something in the kitchen. We had received silver wine glasses for a wedding gift and he had stopped along the way home and bought some wine. He came to the bed and said, "It's time to celebrate." It was such a special time; we had worked so hard to make this dream come true and our reward had come. It makes me giggle now because our great windfall was a school job, the starting wage was $4,800 a year. We were rich.

Seems like life gives us these moments of great joy to help us endure hard times in our life. Jim's brother, Dick, came to our trailer and told us Mom wanted to talk to us. We seldom had phone communication so instantly we knew this had to be bad news. My Dad, my hero and my friend had brain cancer. We made arrangements and headed for Salt Lake City where Dad was to have surgery. We left Bryce with Aunt Anita and Uncle Arch. They later brought him down to Salt Lake to us. He had learned a few new words and how to spit, thanks Uncle Bruce, life on the ranch teaches you all kinds of things. We spent weeks in Salt Lake with Mom and then stayed at the ranch for the rest of the summer.

We rented a house in Plummer that was out in the country and had fields all around it. That fall my brother and Cherie showed up in the stock truck with my horses. We were all emotionally struggling with Dad's sickness. I will never forget this kindness of my brother. He had dropped out of college to come take over the ranch, twenty-four

years old, with a tremendous responsibility.
Jim, Bryce and I loved our little house in the hills.
After years of college life, it was so wonderful to be
by ourselves and have quality time together. We
made lifelong friends in Plummer. An older couple
took us under their wing. Florence and Vern Smith
quickly became our Grandparents. We shared
meals together, went to church together, picnicked
at the lake together. Though we were only in
Plummer two years they were very much a part of
our lives until they went to be with the Lord. All of
our children spent summer vacations with them.
Bryce swears he did enough fishing with Grandpa
in his first 5 years to last a life time. I would phone
up to visit with Jay, and grandma would have to tell
me he didn't want to visit. They didn't miss me half
as much as I missed them. Jim and I tried to
emulate Grandpa and Grandma's simple faith in
Jesus. Their daily lives were an example of humble
service to the Lord.

When Grandpa was dying of lung cancer, I
went up to be with Grandma. One late night he
called to me. He asked if I would close the blind,
because the light was bothering his eyes. It was
pitch dark out. I knew it was Jesus so I ran and got
Grandma. He and Grandma held hands and he
quickly passed from life to life. Several years later, I
went to spend time with Grandma.

She was pretty much blind. I got up early in
the morning and found her out in the kitchen.
When I asked her what she was doing she told me

she was making cookies for the shut-ins. Her son had placed different grits of sand paper on each cupboard so she knew what cupboard she was getting into. Grandma and Grandpa served others every day of their lives. Because Jim had lost his parents at a very young age it was extra special that the Lord brought these wonderful people into our lives to mentor and love us.

The end of that school years Jim had a job with Upward Bound. Upward Bound emerged out of the Economic Act of 1964 in response to the administrations War on Poverty. It was a federally funded program to serve the disadvantaged High school students, and students who neither parent held a bachelor's degree. Jim was very well aware that five years ago he could well have been one of these students, "But for the grace of God, there go I." John Bradford. Upward Bound provided opportunities for students to be able to succeed in their pre-college studies and helped them in their higher education pursuits. Jim was a counselor and worked at the University of Idaho for the summer. Again, trying to find my career calling I headed to South Dakota to work one-on-one with a horse trainer Dad had recommended. I pulled a small camp trailer with our Chevy Nova. With me, I had Bryce and a high school girl to watch Bryce during the summer while I was in class. We followed Jim who was pulling the horse trailer and Stormy, my horse. He got us settled and then headed back to his job. I learned so much that summer. I worked with my horse but Roy Yates, the trainer also had me work with some of his young stock. I felt comfortable after this training in starting young horses and had the knowledge to train them into useful ranch horses.

The ranch we were on was north of Rapid City up in the hills. June 9, 1972 Roy came to my trailer and told me I needed to put my car and trailer into a large barn because they were expecting a large hail storm. I obeyed, but really was not too concerned. Storms at home come and go in a matter of minutes. Two days later we had lived through the Rapid City flood, the most detrimental flood in South Dakota history, and one of the deadliest floods in U. S. history. Hail the size of golf balls pounded the earth for hours and then 15 inches of rain fell in two days. I knew Jim realized we were in the hills, and would not be worried, but what about my parents! Several days after the dirt roads from the ranch were passable, I was able to get to a phone booth and call them. Both Mom and Dad were in tears as I told them we were all OK, they cried, I cried. I hung up and hugged Bryce close to me. On the radio I heard of the destruction and the loss of 238 lives. Several weeks later we went down to look at the devastation, it was heart breaking.

At the end of the summer Jim came back and we all headed home to Carmen. I knew Dad was not in good health and I was desperate to spend some time with him. We pull into the ranch late one night and I run into the house. Mom and Dad were both in bed but I tap on their door and say, "I'm home Daddy." Dad rolled over on his side and reaches out for me and I fall on my knees beside his bed. "Suz, your home!" I hold on to him tightly, I fill myself with his smell, with the feel of his large callused hands, my heart expands and holds him tightly to my soul, he falls back to sleep as I hold him. I thank God for my wonderful father. Believing in my heavenly father has always been easy for me, he must be like my Dad's precious, giving spirit. I back out of the room knowing, I will have tomorrow to fill him in on all I have learned about training horses. Daddy slipped into a coma that night and died several weeks later.

We spent one more wonderful year in Plummer. We had decided to add to our family and were looking forward to the end of May. I was in my last weeks of pregnancy when we got a phone call from my brother. Mom had been helping take cows out to the range, when the lead rope of a horse she was leading got wrapped around her and jerked her off her horse. She had broken her pelvis and was in the hospital. I could tell by the sound of my brother's voice he was at the end of his rope. He kind of hummed and hawed on the phone awhile and then he asked if we could come home for the summer and help take care of Mom and Jim could help him on the ranch. I couldn't travel, I was due to have a baby any day and so we spent an anxious couple of weeks waiting for Jaycob James

Smith. He chose to be different than his brother and decided to enter the earth backwards, May 30, 1973 at Gritman Memorial Hospital. After a pretty intense delivery, I asked the nurse if I could see my son. She said, "Yes, but I want you to know that because he came through the birth canal wrong side up, it flattened his nose, he also has two black eyes, and when they cut your episiotomy they cut the top of his head and he has several stitches." By this time, I have the mad Mom going on, and yell at the nurse, "Bring me my son!" He was born a long tall cowboy, ten pounds and 24 inches long, he looked like he had been out on an all-nighter and had ended up on the raw end of the deal. Jay's take on this story that he has heard a hundred times is; he was born an optimist; he came out face first and he has been looking up ever since.

We moved to Carmen the week after Jay was born. I was delighted to be back on the ranch and thought little of the long hours I put in taking care of a new born baby, caring for my bedridden mother and cooking for the men. There is something about home that just helps you connect. At the end of the summer Jim came in one evening with something on his mind. I waited until we were alone and asked him what he was thinking about. He told me that my brother (whose name is also Jim, so I always refer to him as my brother, to eliminate confusion) has asked him if he would consider staying on the ranch. He offered him shares of the ranch and that they could run it in a partnership. Oh my, huge decision to make. On one hand we had worked so hard for Jim to get through college and were proud of his work as counselor with the Indian children. We loved our friends in Plummer and the life style our job allowed us to have.

On the other hand, my brother needed help. Ranching is a lifestyle that incorporated the entire family. Young, old, hail and hardly are all needed to make the endless jobs come together with a good outcome. Jim had taken to ranching like everything else he had pursued; he was good at it. It made me think of Dad when I told him Jim had asked me to marry him. Dad respected Jim, and felt his virtues, his only concern was my love for ranching. Wouldn't dad be proud of my husband? Our deciding factor was the life style for our children. I could not think of a better gift to give them than the opportunity to be raised on Carmen Creek. To have cousins, aunts and uncles. To be able to run free, and with the support of many, turning into the people God had in mind for each of them.

We decided we would stay on the ranch but would not take shares. My brother had young children of his own who should, one day, inherit the ranch.

I had one stipulation. We needed to have a home of our own. We were able to find a 14x70 foot trailer, it was a palace compared to our pink Kit, we moved it onto the ranch.

Chapter 6

18 Years on the Ranch
1973-1991

A cowboy's heart is strong and faithful,
A cowboy's heart is true,
The love you feel from a cowboy's heart
Not wondering and always for you.
Laurie Morgan

Life on the ranch fell into its steady rhythm. Fall: get cattle off the range, ween the calves, ship the calves to market, preg-check the cows. Winter: feed cows, calving time, constantly check for sick livestock. Spring: Brand calves, turn cows out to range, clean ditches, farm, irrigate. Summer: ride the range and move cows, irrigate morning and night, hay, harvest.

Working together as a family gives you a connection. These next couple of years were great. Finally, life seemed to get back on an even keel again. One of the joys of ranch life is you get to spend so much time together as a family. We would all go build fence and have a picnic. We would irrigate grain and work as a team getting the water down each furrow. The whole family was in the hay field with their own responsibilities. The joy of the summer was heading to cow camp, 16 miles up in the mountains from the ranch. We camped, laughed, moved cows, laughed and bonded as an extended family.

From 1962 to 1974 cattle prices were on a steady increase from 20 cents a pound to 47 cents a pound. Things were really starting to look good in the cattle business. Then in 1975 the cattle market dropped 16 cents per pound, most ranchers were lucky to get 30 cents a pound that year. Ranchers receive one income, calves, and they get this income once a year. Thank God we had decided not to take shares of the ranch because with this market it could not support more than one family. There was a part time school counseling job open in Salmon and Jim applied and got the job. As the cattle market continued to decline, he worked more and more in town. Jim still worked full time on the ranch during the summers and helped with calving and working the cattle.

We were content with our life on the ranch and decided to make it permanent and build a house. Mom gave us a couple of acres at the very bottom of the ranch. Actually, she gave us a piece of heaven. Carmen Creek runs near our home site and the Bitterroot Mountains tower above us. We are surrounded by Cottonwood and Aspen trees and a spring bubbles past our front door. When I say we had decided to build a house I meant that "literally". We had never built anything in our lives but with optimistic youth on our side, plenty of energy, and Uncle Jim's book, "Build Your House for $4,000," we moved forward. I started drawing house plans and Jim started digging for a foundation. Our plan was an open design 35x40 feet on the bottom floor with half of that being open beam and the other half had an upstairs that opened out over the living room. Seems like the story of our lives, big plans, perseverance and big accomplishments. When you are walking hand and hand with the Lord, listening, and then being obedient, you will find that God works in ordinary, everyday ways. Over and over we witnessed His help as we were building a home for our family.

The first obstacle was the foundation. We did not have an adequate road to the building spot to bring in a cement truck. The truck parked on the hill above the house and Jim, Dave and my brother wheelbarrowed cement down to form the footings. Then Jim and I built a cinder block foundation. Back breaking work, sweat drenching, mosquito miserable work. We were just finishing the foundation when we received a call from southern Idaho saying the logs we had ordered could not be delivered. Devastated, but not down, we waited on the Lord. Within days we got a call from Uncle Frank who was finishing a logging sale in the Wisdom, Montana area. Part of his contract said he had to clear cut the area when he was finished logging. He knew we were planning on building a log house and offered to give us the standing dead that were still on the sale, this saved us hundreds of dollars. Bryce, age 5, Jim and I headed over and set up camp. Uncle Frank told us he had a two-week deadline to be out of that area. Jim taught Bryce how to measure the size of tree he wanted. Bryce tied plastic ribbons on the trees, Jim sawed them down and I pulled them into a pile using our Ford Bunco. One early morning Jim went out to start cutting and it started to snow, he headed to a brush pile to seek shelter, within the pile was a coat. Jim put it on and kept on working. We were getting near to our goal of 200 trees when Jim ran out of saw gas. We were miles from any kind of town and on a tight time line. On his way back to camp he found a gas can full of saw gas. We worked hard and had enough logs for our house. The last night at camp I wander out among the stars, thanking God for supplying us with our needs. I heard his voice speak, "Many little feet will patter through your home." Really!!

We pulled camp and headed down to the Big Hole Battle field to use their phone to call the trucks we had lined up, from Hamilton, Montana, to come haul our logs. They said we could not use the phone, we drove on into Wisdom, Montana. There we saw a little saw mill and stopped to visit. We hired the Wilkie brothers in Wisdom to haul the logs to their mill and had them flattened on two sides. They charged us half what the mill in Hamilton had quoted us. Jim used the ranch stock truck to deliver them to Carmen.

Meanwhile, Jim and I were busy building the floor. At that time there was a saw mill in Salmon and we were able to purchase rough cut

2x10's very reasonably. We used this to frame the floor and also to surface the floor. We had a solid base to start building our logs on. Jim really enjoyed laying the logs, and he was good at it. Every six or eight feet he would drill down through the logs, a foot or so, and then pound rebar in to make the walls stable. My heart smiles when I remember him straddling those logs with the big power drill and foot long bit. My man.

Mom was like our cheerleader. Every afternoon when she came home from school, she would bring us a treat. One time, in the fall before we had the roof on, she stopped by. We were looking a little defeated because we had received several inches of snow. She climbed the ladder to our second floor and started shoveling, bless her soul, she believed in us. Mom also bought the windows for our house. When we got the walls all up, Jim spent days sitting on top of the wall pondering how to build the roof. As he was sitting on the top log of the corner of our living room, a plan came to him. He hauled a small log up and started lifting it. Mom and I were below, all of the sudden I could see Jim's plan would allow us to have a wall of windows with angled windows above, in the living room, encompassing the Bitterroot peaks. "I lift my eyes to the mountains; from whence shall my strength come? My help comes from the Lord." Psalm 121

Jim's brother Dick, an electrician, came and wired the house for the cost of the supplies. We hired a plumber. We spent $18,000 on our 2,000 square foot home and did not have to borrow a penny.

Jim and Bryce, Jay and I were living in a camp trailer while we built the house. Needless to say, we spend every available minute working on the house. We moved in with a tarp for a front door and a 50-gallon barrel wood stove for heat. Grandma and Grandpa Smith came down to help us that spring. Grandpa took a look around and said, "I am going to put in your front door." That first winter we burnt 10 cord of wood. That spring the 50-gallon barrel was thrown out the back door and replaced by wood stoves. Cherie came down to help me wallpaper the bathroom and Jay and Brandon both about 2 ½ years old were outside playing. Cherie and I were laughing a goofing around having fun. We looked out the window and both boys had climbed into the 50-gallon barrel. We went running out the door as two very black boys came crawling back out.

I sewed a large tapestry of our home, it hung in our living room for years. Sewn across the top were the words, "Because the Lord is our Strength," proclaiming to all who entered our home from whence our strength comes. Jim and I have raised our 10 children in this home. We have welcomed foster children and grandchildren. Now with my school attached to our home we have a constant patter of little feet in our, "Home."

I was steadily breaking and training horses at this time. I worked our ranch horses but I also brought in outside horses to work. Many of the horses came to me with bad habits, intense fears and trust issues. After several years of this kind of work I just turned back to working with our own stock of young horses we raised and bought. My skills are better suited to working with young stock, gaining their trust, and spending hundreds of hours doing ground work. By the time I swing on a horse for the first time they know the voice commands of come, whoa and back. They know how to turn on their hinds, on their rear legs, tie, and are comfortable with having their feet worked on.

From the ground I teach them how to rein and then use that skill to teach them to drive. I saddle the colt and attach a long-line to their bridle, thread the lines through the stirrups, to keep them off the ground, I walk at their shoulder and then inch back further and further until I am walking behind them. I repeatedly saddle, harness and sack them out.

I begin all this when they are about six months old, by the time they are two I'm comfortable to step into the saddle. On, I reteach them everything I have introduced to them from the ground. After we have covered all the basics it is then time for hours of wet saddle blankets. I ride them in all kinds of terrain, getting them familiar with trees, crossing ditches, sand, rocks steep hills, and sharp descents. I ride them on windy days, snowy days, rain, sun and cold. The first rides I do not demand anything of them than to be responsive to my leg pressure for their direction.

Second, back in the coral, I step up my demand to react to my leg pressure by turning them in large circles, and then figure eights. When they are responding nicely, I ask the same response at a trot. Finally, gentle rides behind cattle, praying there won't be any need for a buckaroo. Two years of this type of consistent, patient training, prayer for no major accident, produces a valuable asset for the ranch.

Most of our horses with their good breeding and training turn out to be average or better horses but occasionally there is a cayuse. When your path crosses a cayuse, you are best to be shed of him quickly. Letting pride rule, thinking you can win in the end, leads to a wreck. Seems like all of us have had to learn this lesson the hard way.

On the other hand, sometimes God hands you a horse so outstanding, they become an instant treasure. Talk to any old cowboy and he will name you a handful of good horses he has had in his day.

Next month I will be seventy years old. Jim and I are spending the month of February in Nevada riding two green colts. Jim has become a real hand and if I feel I need a little help I gladly pass the reins over to him.

Good horses are rare as buried treasures,
It's a blue moon cast his light on more than one.
A band as strong as any chain between man and
equine beast.
Steady as the rising of the sun.
If a cowboy get a good one.
A mount as right as rain
Honest as a mothers tears of joy.
You cannot help but wonder when a great horse is
put down
If there's a place up yonder waiting for cowboys?
So I'm building my Ramada up in heaven.
I swear I hear their hoof beats in the sky
The Lord will hold my cavy till they've carved a
stone for me
And when I get there I can saddle up and ride.

We are so thankful that Jay entered the world a big health baby. I have pictures of his sweet little fat rolls from his chin down to his ankles. However, by the time he was 6 months old he was critically ill. He started losing weight at an alarming rate and could not keep anything on his stomach. For the next three years, every time he ate, he threw-up. Jim and I were frantic and had him to doctors all over the northwest, we even took him to Mexico. The doctors in Salmon had no idea. One wanted to operate. When I ask him why? His answer was maybe they could find something. We were sent to Missoula, Montana, and to Seattle, Washington. In desperation we headed to

Mexico. All told us he was very ill, but none could tell us why. Someone gave us the name of a doctor in Provo, Utah, finally a glimmer of hope. He explained to us he thought it was an allergy but did not represent itself on the skin or repertory system. Jay's reaction caused an inflammation in his brain. This inflammation caused the nausea, migraine headaches, and extreme fatigue to the point of near paralysis. With Dr. Remington's encouragement we moved forward. Through trial, error and illumination we were starting to pin point some foods we knew made him sicker. Months later we realized the common ingredient was "Corn." Sounds simple to illuminate corn from a diet, not so at all. Corn is the cheapest feed for beef, sheep, pigs, and fowl. He could not eat anything that had eaten corn. Corn is the cheapest sweetener and is virtually in every canned or frozen product in the store. Corn is the cheapest starch, it is in table salt, backing powder, sugar and medicine capsules. You get the idea, to eliminate corn was an enormous undertaking. Thankfully, I was a stay at home mom because producing food for our family became my full-time job. We milked a cow that was fed on grass hay so we could have milk, and butter. We raised her calf so we could have beef. I raised chickens and did not feed them commercial feed so we could have eggs and chicken. I raised an enormous garden and canned and froze fruit and vegetables. I had my routine like the good old days; wash on Monday, clean on

Tuesday, bake on Wednesday, churn on Thursday, cook three meals a day from scratch. My work was good, busy, and gave me great satisfaction.

During this time, we also realized he was very sensitive to chemical smells. Hair spray, perfume, fabric softener, the list goes on and on.

When Jay was 5 years old, we went back to college so Jim could pick up a specialist degree to be a school administrator. While we were there Jay got very ill. I took him to the doctor and found out he had pneumonia. Jim and I spent an hour educating the doctor, who happened to believe us, of why Jay could not be put in the hospital. Of course, the food, but the capsules medicine is in and the cleaning products. We knew one unintentional slip and we would lose our son. My mind cries when I remember our terribly ill, very thin, even more fragile son, as Jim carries him in his arms and places him in his bed. We would take the medicine out of the capsules and place them on a piece of bread, mash it up and get him to swallow it down.

Another time I got a phone call from school that Jay had passed out and I needed to come get him. He was in middle school and they were dissecting frogs. When the teacher opened the container of frogs, the formaldehyde smell from across the room, caused Jay to pass out and fall backwards off his science stool. The next year during Christmas break the school put in new carpet. After the new year when Jay went back to school, he became so ill, we had to take him out of that building for the rest of the year. New carpet is filled with formaldehyde. You do not rush a child with Jay's condition to the emergency room, it would just compound the illness, you take him home and comfort and pray.

Jay had a bedroom in the upstairs of our home and Jim put in a fresh air system that allowed air flow. When Jay would either eat something or come in contact with a chemical, he would go to his room, turn off the light, ask to be alone, and lie there in agony for days at a time until the body had an opportunity to cleanse itself.

As we gained skills in regulating his environment and his intake his health started to improve. He has the spirit of a lion. He never complained when he couldn't have things other kids had or when he just physically could not keep up. As I mentioned before he is an optimist, has always had a clear vison of his future, and with his hand in Gods, has made it all come true.

By this time Jim and I were really wanting to add a member to our family. I really, really wanted a little girl. One of my mother's favorite sayings was, "A boy is your boy until he finds a wife but a girl is your girl for the rest of your life." I longed for a daughter. I had been dealing with endometriosis, a disorder in which tissue that normally lines the uterus grows outside the uterus, inflaming the fimbria, which pick up the egg and transport it into the fallopian tube, causes swelling and scarring so the egg may not reach its destination. Dr. Simmons said the disease was so advanced he doubted I could conceive. So, we prayed and tried, and prayed for a baby girl. January 25, 1977 Beth Suzanne Smith bounded into our lives. A gift with a marvelous spirit. A spirit that imbedded itself into to each of our hearts.

Looking back, you recognize priceless nuggets in life. In our late twenties Jim and I helped establish an interdenominational Bible study. People from a variety of religious backgrounds met each week to discuss the Bible. We had no leader, the host each week chose the scripture. We praised the lord, sang songs, discussed openly and prayed widely. We organized interdenominational church camps, children choirs and youth activities. I look back, realizing this was the "70's," when the hippies were practicing peace and free love. Perhaps the breaking down of church walls was our way of protesting, our way of examining the shortfalls of the past, our desire to have a more harmonious world.

Is was at this time Jim and I read Nine O'clock in the Morning by Dennis Bennett. We were struck, we now knew what was missing in our walk. Jim and I were baptized in the Holy Spirit and began our sanctification as believers. The Lord cleanses people one spot at a time. Your acceptance to the will of God is a starting point. The cleansing is a lifelong process. This experience was our baby step in developing a personal, nonreligious, faith in God.

I was raised in a mixed religion home. My father, a man of great spirit, was a Mormon. My mother, who had a profound personal faith, was a Protestant. I never remember a religious argument between them. I attended Primary and I attended Sunday school. The Methodist women group met in our home and the Mormon ward teachers were welcome in our home. Nevertheless, I was always fighting a conflict. Was one right and the other wrong? Could they both be right? What if they were both wrong?

I chose as a young adult to build a personal relationship with Jesus not based on any religious doctrine. I believe that Jesus is the son of God. I believe Jesus lived to teach me how to live. I believe he died for my sins, I believe he sent the Holy Spirit to me that I may have communication with Him. I believe it is my responsibility on earth to serve and in order to serve I must know how to listen to the Lord's leadings.

Hopefully, our walk with the Lord is a constant maturation. It includes a desire to listen more closely, a strength to cleanse more deeply, an obedience if convicted, or a willingness to reach beyond our comfort zone. I need a quiet time with the Lord every day, I do not want to have any time restraints. I also need a place of solitude, I want to feel free to sing, praise or scream. I want to enter my place knowing I have come here to commune with my maker. I read the scripture-ponder-meditate-question-dig deeper. I ask the Holy Spirit to help me understand, how does this apply to my life? What do you want me to do? In Jesus name I ask in faith to be able to perceive the will of God. Not my will but His!!

In order to accomplish this, I am reminded of I Samuel 3:7-11 "Speak, Lord for thy servant is listening." What is a good listener? How can I improve my listening skills? Through the help of Charles Stanley, I have determined a good listener must listen:

1. Expectantly
2. Quietly
3. Patiently
4. Actively
5. Confidently
6. Humbly
7. Openly
8. Attentively
9. Carefully
10. Submissively
11. Gratefully
12. Reverently

Constantly, I am at war with the old man. "I am perfectly sure about this fact: if I could expel all pride, vanity, self-righteousness, self-seeking, desire for applause, honor, and promotion—if by some divine power I should be utterly emptied of all that, the Spirit would come as a rushing wind to fill me." A. J. Gordon.

I am encouraged by the growth of my spirit; I am comforted to daily realize I am a work in progress. I am amazed to be able to celebrate great victories. My faith in God has been a solid rock it times of overwhelming sorrow.

Jim has had a remarkable career, while we were in Salmon, he went from part time counselor, to special education director to the superintendent of the Salmon schools for eleven years. Later we moved to the Boise area and he was Chief Certification Officer and Executive Director of Professional Standards Commission. He finished his career climb as the Deputy Superintendent of Finance of Education for Idaho. Jim is a man of service, in his retirement he has been superintendent of the Leadore School, a fire man, an EMT, a deputy sheriff, a fire commissioner, financial coordinator of Upper Carmen School, and helped the Salmon Schools as in interim superintendent for a year. He plows roads for all the neighbors, works cows, with a twinkle in his eye, marries and buries community members. He is a wonderful father and a devoted grandfather. He is my best friend and soul mate. I miss him the moment he leaves my side and am overjoyed each time I see him return, it doesn't matter if he has been gone 5 minutes or 5 days. Jim did not just financially take good care of his family, he surrounded it in warmth, security, steadfastness, devotion, commitment, and wisdom. When the world goes wrong, who does his family, friends and strangers call, Jim? You know he will listen, understand, encourage and help. He is the most thoughtful person I have ever known.

Financially stable, three wonderful children, a lovely home; how can we best serve the Lord? One sentence in scripture bites at my heart each time I read it: "Religion that God our Father accepts as pure and faultless is that: to look after orphans and widows in their distress." James 1:27 Because Jim knows all too well the life of an orphan and I have the desire to nurture we start the conversation about adoption. Jim and I have a dedication to help the helpless. We have an unquenchable desire to love the unloved, comfort the struggling, and to satisfy the needs of children. It seems much more than a desire, it is a driving force in our lives. We investigate the possibility of adopting within the United States and soon find we are not eligible because we have three children of our own. Undeterred, we start searching international adoption. We were delighted to find The World Association for Children and Parents (WACAP). It is a non-profit, domestic and international adoption agency established in 1976. They have placed 12,000 children into loving homes across the United States and provided humanitarian aid to over 250,000 children worldwide. WACAP's mission is a family for every child.

We make contact with WACAP and they start sending us pictures of children that are in need of a home. We wait on the Lord to show us which child is to be a part of our family. One sad little Korean toddler speaks to our hearts February 19, 1982 and we start the adoption process. It is impossible to express our family's excitement, as we press against the glass in the Seattle Washington airport, waiting to see the first glimpse of our new family member. The moment Lee, Eun Hye is placed in my arms, I am engulfed with the strongest kind of love. I understand the vastness of this responsibility, but with God's strength I am assured our family can give this lost lamb comfort.

We name her Rebekah Lee Smith. Because her birth date is unknown, we give February 19, 1981, the day we chose her for our own. We think Becky was about 1 ½ years old when she came home. She was malnourished, her body was covered with running sores, she would just lay on the floor and rock back and forth and scream. When we sat up to meals, she would gorge herself and then when I would but her down from the high-chair she would grab handfuls of food to take with her. Physically she was very delayed, she could sit up but could not crawl. The kids spent hours with her on the floor playing with her and showing her how to crawl and held her so she could put weight on her legs. Socially, she was a terrified, wild little animal. In time she started to respond to her safe, comfortable environment. This pudgy cheeked toddler started imitating all of our actions but seemed unable to communicate with us. We assumed it was because of the language change.

Sitting in the waiting room of the audiologist with my two-year-old daughter, I start becoming uneasy because we have been waiting a lengthy time since Becky's hearing test. I am here because we believe there is a possibility that Becky might have some hearing loss. Several weeks ago, we bought the kids some ducks and Jim came up behind Becky and held the quacking duck to her ear, she doesn't even know he is there. She has been in our home six months and she has no language. The door opens, I know from my first look at the Doctor's face, she has bad news. Profoundly Deaf--, Deaf--, my alert, intelligent little girl. I feel desperately alone. It is like I am an actress in some daytime soap opera and yet I don't know how to play the role. I gather my child into my arms, I hold her tight, as if someone is trying to take her away from me. In a crazy way I feel like this child of mine has died. The expectations I had for her are melting away and I can no longer visualize her future. I walk to the Ear Nose Throat Specialist in a haze, knowing that he will "fix" this problem. Never speak--, never achieve more than a 3rd grade education, what is the doctor saying. These words numb me but yet are screaming in my head like scorching fire.

Jim and I just could not take "never," for an answer. We started researching educational programs for deaf children and soon found out it was like arguing religion. There were two distinct camps. Total Communication, which uses sign language and speech. And Oral/Auditory that uses residual hearing and teaches the deaf child to speak. We chose the oral/auditory approach. In this program you train the deaf child to use what hearing they have. It is necessary to have hearing aids that are proper for the child's loss. An FM system is worn by parents or teachers, this system allows that person's voice to be transmitted directly to the hearing aid. We took the whole family to Los Angles to attend the John Tracy Clinic. That summer oral/auditory teachers worked with Becky. Bryce, Jay and Beth attended classes for siblings and Jim and I attended classes for parents. We came home with a plan. We hired an oral/auditory speech specialist, Mary States, to come to our home every six months, she would work with Becky for a couple days and leave me with extensive lessons plans.

Both of us sitting on the bathroom counter and looking into the mirror I would say a word, show her a picture of the word, she would stare intently at my lips and mimic how my lips moved. Her first spontaneous word was "up." We started developing a word list and were delighted with the progress she was making but I was still confused about how to teach her the flow of language. By this point of time there was not a doubt in my mind that she was very intelligent. I found the Dormac reading series that was written for the deaf, it was written using the sight word approach and was very repetitive. The other kids were all in school and so Becky and spent hours each morning with her reading. By the time she was three years old she was an effective reader and her world started to open up.

Public school was a challenge, but she was a brave soul. She was different on two counts being oriental and being deaf. It didn't take long until she was way past a third-grade level of education, academically she began to soar, graduating as valedictorian of her high school class and summa cum laude from Gallaudet University.

Bryce was three years old when we moved to the ranch and the years flew by. Ten years later I was in the kitchen cooking breakfast crying my eyes out. Bryce comes down the stairs and ask me what is wrong. I turn to him and tell him I do not know how to be the mother of a thirteen-year-old. Bryce in is matter of fact way says, "Well, Mom I don't know how to be a thirteen-year-old either, I guess we will just figure it out." And we did. With mutual respect the teen years went sweeping by.

I was not prepared for this next phase in my life when my children start leaving the nest. In the spring of '88 Bryce join the United States Army and left soon after he graduated from high school. Honest to God, I thought I would die. I was like an old mother cow, each night I would head up to the end of our driveway where I had last seen Bryce and wail, the separation was so painful. In time the Lord was able to reassure me that though he is no longer by my side he is forever in my heart.

We stayed very active with WACAP, several other families in our community also adopted children and we would have international picnics, we celebrated each time a new child came home.

Jim and I felt our family was complete. However, we continued to get pictures of children waiting for a forever home. One of the pictures so touched my heart. A five your old little Korean boy, who at the age of three, had been found wandering the streets of Seoul, Korea. He had been in an orphanage for two years. They had "alert" on his picture because he was diagnosed with Failure to Thrive. He had given up; his little soul could no longer cope with the uncertainty of life. I placed his picture on the fridge and prayed for him each day. His picture had been up for a week or so when Jim noticed it and ask me about the child. I read Jim Suh, Kung Young's life profile. Jim's instant reply was, "Let's bring him home."

Have you ever planted a little seed? You are not sure what kind of seed it is, so you wait impatiently for it to begin to sprout and grow. This is like every little child. For some, the seeds are plump and ready to grow immediately, while others have been abused, and the seed is withered or damaged. All children need care, but some need more individual attention than others. Because of your great concern for your seed, you give it all the care this tiny life needs in order to give it the best chance for success. As the root matures and sinks into the consistent foundation of love, it begins to send out a more advanced root system, building confidence in others around it. With solid roots the stem boldly appears. The child is standing freely, secure and ready to bloom. As each petal of the bloom begins to open the child's talents are revealed to you, one at a time.

Thomas Daniel Smith was a damaged seedling. Jim, Beth, Becky and I flew to Seattle Washington to get him June 19, 1988, Father's Day. The moment we were introduced he attached to Jim. Years later he explained to me he had many mothers, women in the orphanage, but he had never had a father. I had recently had surgery and was unable to lift and had limited energy and so Beth stepped up as mother. Beth and Tom became very close, and retained that inseparability. Tom learned the English language in three months and started school with his peers. His talents were amazing. Each evening I would sit in awe watching this child. He could fold paper, cut out a design and have a three-dimensional figure. One night he was busy cutting and when I looked up the paper had been turned into a covered wagon and two horses pulling it. He was equally talented in drawing. We have his art hanging in our home. Put perhaps his greatest talent, music. His violin filled our home with majestic sounds, by the time he was 11 years old he was playing in concerts.

He, like his sister Becky, was very impressed with food. One day at the grocery store I bought a large box of oranges, he turned to me and said in an astonished voice, "Are all of those for us?" At night when I tucked him into bed, he would throw his arms around my neck and say, "I love you Mom Smith." The original damaged seedling is now producing a tremendous bloom.

But always it was his Dad who lit his eyes with love and admiration. When he was 11 years old an English assignment was to write about his favorite character, he wrote:

My Character

I think my dad is a real character because he rides his motorcycle in the winter to work in Boise. He also mixes cereals together and he likes it. He likes to mix hot chocolate powder with vanilla ice cream. He likes to dance but, he dances too fast. My Dad carries an umbrella on his arm all the time. He likes dogs but he doesn't pet them. He likes to get stuck in the mud with his motorcycle. When he talks about one thing, he changes the subject to something else totally different.

All my children are doing well in school, and though I am plenty busy at home, I have time on my hands. That old haunted feeling comes to visit again, what does the Lord want me to be? I know my cup is full and I appreciate the many blessings that have been sent my way, but nevertheless I have to address this uneasiness in my soul. I take a day to myself and saddle up, one fine spring day.

Once again, I turn Willow out the high pasture gate and allow her to take her time climbing the steep sage brush hill and mount the ridge. Horseback my soul is at peace and my Spirit is sensitive to God's creation all around me. I have a vast view of our ranch and the valley below. I am surrounded by lupine, Indian paintbrush, balsam root and bitterroot. The pungent earth is alive with the scents of Spring. We pass Badger Springs, and follow the stream through the blooming pussy willows. God is singing in my inner soul, the world is breaking out in newness of life, He is preparing me for the message he has for my heart.

I side hill to my final destination, my secret place. I allow Willow to roam around, knowing she would never leave me. I center myself on a small patch of green and silence my heart. I've brought a picnic and enjoy my snack while being chorused by a flock of blackbirds. Then I lie on my back and look deep into the heavens and thank God for my abundant blessings. Time passes and perhaps I even dozed off. "I want you to be a teacher." I bolt myself upright, not believing the words I had heard. Are you kidding me! You know better than anyone how torturous school was for me. I'm still recovering from the name calling and the belittling, that withered my spirit, all those years ago. I have no desire to be anything like most of the teachers of my past. Why would I ever want to be in that environment? "So, other little children do not have to go through what you did, you would understand, you would make sure they were successful." I lie back down thinking on this, I knew God would never ask me to do something I was unable to do. I'm just starting to come to terms with this when He says, "I want you to teach reading." God! It took me 20 years to learn how to read. The word I "can't," was just about to come out of my mouth when I realized I taught Becky how to read. "I want you to love Me, I want you to be the best wife you can be, I want you to be the best mother you can be, and I want you to teach children how to read."

I climbed back on my horse and aimlessly wander through the hills. I am trying to come to terms with what this would mean to my family. The closest University to Carmen is 150 miles away. Over the years I have gathered over 100 credits but they aren't in any special area of study. I am 40 years old, and school had never been my friend. By the time I swing off at the barn I am exhausted. That evening, after the kids are in bed, I tell Jim about my day. He instantly encourages me and reassures me that we can make all the logistics work. That month I travel around to our closest Universities to see who had a good reading program and who would accept my credits. Idaho schools did not have what I was looking for. Someone suggested Utah State University. I knew instantly it was a fit. There reading program was exactly what I was looking for and they accepted every one of my credits. Visiting with a counselor, I discovered in 12 months I could have degrees in

Early Childhood, Early Childhood Special Education and K-8 Education.

Beth and Jay stayed in Carmen with Jim and Becky and Tom came with me. We lived in married student housing. It just so happens that our next-door neighbors were Korean, we became good friends. It was so wonderful for the kids to have exposure to their natural heritage. It was a long year living apart and a lot of hard work. School work seemed easier for me, of course I still had my limitations but I had learned how to work around them. I had a very successful year and it was celebrated by having my family and my oldest sister and mother come to my graduation. As I walked down the aisle, I watch the smiling face of my mother, in my heart I was thanking her for always believing in me, always lifting me up. Mom had the ability to see a "me" I was unable to see, her love and determination lite my way.

Salmon's stable economics was based on the cattle industry and the logging industry. In the 1980's the logging industry took a major hit. New federal regulations made it very difficult for loggers to buy timber sales. One by one families started moving out of our valley. The final straw was when the Salmon Saw Mill was no longer able to hold on and had to close down. This steady exit of citizen took a tremendous impact on all the business in Salmon, not excluding the school. In a three-year period of time the school population went from 1,800 to 1,300 and continued to fall. Jim, as superintendent was in the position of putting forth a reduction in force. This is never pleasant and the after-affect lasts years. He diligently worked them through this finical crisis and got them on solid ground.

It was time for Jim and I to move on. We both applied for jobs in the Boise area and within a short period of time started a whole new chapter in our lives.

Chapter 7

South Idaho

1. The most important thing in your life is your relationship with God.
2. Obey God, and leave all the consequences to him.
3. God will move heaven and earth to reveal His will to you if you really want to know it and do it.
4. God will provide for all of your needs.
5. God will protect you.
   S. D. Gordon

For God to direct us away from Carmen was an immense blow. Leaving our home, our family and friends and especially the ranch life style, not knowing if we would be able to return, took a tremendous amount of faith and a strong will to follow where we had been directed. We were moving our country kids into city life; we were moving Jim and I into city life. Together, we worked to make this transition a bridge not a burden. We had a choice to see it as a heavy weight that would lug us down into bitterness or we could see it as a bridge that would be the conduit to our next phase of service.

Increasing the internal struggle were two facts. Jay was a senior in high school and had made the decision to stay in Carmen and finish his senior year. Also, my Mom was very ill, we all knew she was losing her battle with cancer. I had lived within an easy walk of my mother the last 18 years and we were very dependent on each other. Obedience is often times very onerous, the conflict with in my Spirit was wrenching. I spent late night hours walking the hills, crying out to God to help me be supportive of this move. I knew it was instrumental in Jim's advancement and for my own opportunity to teach. One comfort, we did not have to sell our home and were able to rent it out. This gave us the hope that someday, perhaps Carmen would again be our home.

We had determined that we could not live in the city and started looking for housing outside of the Boise area. One real estate ad trumpeted that the house had a perfect view of the mountains. Having lived smack dab at the foot of the Bitterroot Mountains nearly all my life this caught my attention. The house sat on three acres and so I would be able to bring a horse or two but I was so disappointed when I realized you almost needed binoculars to see the mountains. I must adjust, adjust I told myself daily as we signed the contract.

This move had many positive aspects for our children. Beth was in ninth grade when we moved, she had been playing piano since grade-school and had really excelled. We were able to find her a music teacher at the university, her abilities bloomed and grew. Our Asian children, Becky and Tom fit right into Greenhurst Elementary School. The diverse population made them no longer an oddity. Becky was able to get quality interpreters and became acquainted with other deaf children. Tom took violin lesson from a gifted Japanese woman, June Otomi. Interesting note; (Mrs. Otomi's family were placed in the Minidoka internment camp during WWII.) They had a wonderful relationship, her gentle encouragement allowed him to sail. Our shy, introverted, sweet boy was soon playing concerts that made your soul soar.

Jim smoothly moved into his new position as Chief Certification Officer and Executive Director of Professional Standards Commission for the Idaho Department of Education. This position required a great deal of travel and over the years he traveled all over the United States. He finished his career climb as the Deputy Superintendent of Finance of Education for Idaho. He worked hand-in-hand with the State Superintendent of instruction to make the school budget for the state of Idaho. He then was responsible to navigate this budget through legislature. It was an intense job, high stakes for every school in Idaho.

I had obtained my teaching certificate the year before we moved and was looking for a teaching position that would fit my calling to work with underprivileged children. I came upon a job description: Needed, a person to create a school for abused and abandoned children. This was my introduction to Hope House. Hope House exists to provide a home for children who are emotionally impaired, developmentally disabled, and/or come from disrupted adoptions or dysfunctional families. Hope House began with a promise made by a little girl; herself abandoned and a victim of abuse, neglect and family dysfunction; who vowed that someday, she would make a home where children like herself could be loved and cared for. Donna Velvick was able to make her childhood promise come to life. For the past 33 years she has given a home to children." The ten years I was actively involved with Hope House there were never less than 50 children finding refuge in Donna's comfort. I am humbled to the core when I visualize the impact of her ministry. A profound Christian, she has depended totally on God to bring her vision to fruition.

Up until 1991 she had been sending her children to public school, oftentimes with devastating results. It had become clear to her that she also needed to provide quality education for her family. Their home was in an old school house and beside it stood and old Grange Hall. The Grange Hall was to be the school. I walked into that building that had been, itself, abandoned for years. It was covered in layers of dirt, flies and colder than a barn. I take a deep breath, holding tightly to

God's apron strings, and repeating to myself.
Hold on,
Don't run,
One step more.

       I accepted the job. I dove into cleaning the hall, recalling my mother's many stories of teaching in an old Grange Hall, she rode a horse to school, built her own fires, hauled her own water, and taught grades 1-8. O.K., I tell myself, if Mom could do it, so could I. I suggest we divide the building in half and have the k-8 on one side and the 9-12 on the other. Donna gets volunteer help and that project is quickly accomplished. Because we have no furniture, they build individual cubicles on the walls. The building was the least of my concerns. We have no supplies and no money. Remember, I had never taught a day of school in my life. I had so much self-doubt, it almost filled the room. I certainly had never written a curriculum K-12th grade. Donna hired a high school teacher and we made the decision to have them use an established, Christian based, pace program. The high school teacher's responsibility would be to monitor them through the curriculum. Meanwhile, it would give us time to get our elementary children academically successful, and prepare them for a more vigorous course of study when they were high school age.

The first day of school I had 27 students ages from 5 to 16, almost none had ever had the opportunity to learn to read or do simple math. All had experienced negative school experiences. Okay God I whisper, help me to show them your peace. I had gotten very good at oral reading, and with my drama background I could make a book come alive. As they enter, I have them sit on the floor around me and before introductions or anything, I start reading <u>Old Yeller</u>. The commotion starts to settle down and one by one I can see that they are starting to plug into the story line. By the end of the first chapter they are with me, I continue for an hour. I look up from my reading and give them a few moments and then ask them to tell me about what we have just read. One-by-one, hands go up and we have our first literary discussion. Feeling the comfort in the room I quietly introduce myself and assign seats for each student. I had a list of group activities for the day in order to give myself an opportunity to informally assess their abilities and their special needs. The lack of reading ability, even in the older students, led to creating project-based activities and oral history. Within in a few short weeks I had groups working independently while I worked with ability equal groups. My communication with the Lord was minute by minute. The Helper is a teacher above all teachers and I needed that direct connect to meet the needs of these children. I was the first to admit there was no way I could accomplish this task on my own.

Day by day, some plans working, some falling flat on their face, children started feeling themselves grow, and this growth brought about smiles of success.

It makes my mind cry to remember some of the children I worked with. One impertinent young lady was asked to stay after school. When all the kids left, she marched up to me, put her hands on her hips, and said, "You cannot do anything to me that has not already been done." My heart sunk to the floor; I knew it was true. "Yes, I can," I slowly respond, "I can love you." She stared at me in disbelief, we talked about her behavior in the classroom and I excused her. The next morning her attitude had improved and she offered to stay after school and help me clean. Another little boy had actually been raised in a cage. He had stood on his tip toes so many years holding on to the cage he was unable to set his feet down flat. He was a wild animal. I taught him his alphabet by sitting on the floor with my legs wrapped around him to keep him in one place. I worked with children that had been sexually abused at very young ages, children who had been beaten to the point of permanent brain damage, fetal alcohol children, and children who had been adopted for ill gain. The list goes on-and-on, because every child that has ever lived at Hope House, has their own horrific story. I conditioned myself to give 100% when I was at work, but mentally turn it off when I went home. Some days I was better at this than others, but I had to survive in order to give them as much as I could.

The classroom could turn volatile with the least provocation. I was always on high alert to intervene at the first sign of contention. One of the job requirements was to pass a self-defense class. I seldom had to use this but on occasion it was necessary for me to take a child down to prevent harm to themselves or to others. Even when the waters were calm, you could feel the undertone of sadness, profound hurt, loneliness, desperation. Dejection is overwhelming, and healing, in the best of environments is a long hard road.

This teaching experience has been invaluable to me. It taught me the need to meet their social and emotional needs before I could expect much from them academically. It taught me that every child deserves an opportunity to be successful, no matter how small the steps are. It also taught me that children have an innate ability to love their parents; even if the parents have not been kind or responsible, have been horrible role models, lack compassion or the capacity to love anyone but themselves, if even that. The reason children crumble, wither up on the inside and their little Spirits dim into nothingness, is because they have been cut off from parental adoration. Who wants to live if there is no one to live for?

I am proud of the ten years I spent at Hope House. When I was needed elsewhere, I was able to train a teaching staff to continue. I go back and visit and am blessed, that the school I started twenty-eight years ago, is still giving quality education to the children who have the privilege of living at Hope House. Donna Velvick, is one of my hero's, thank you Jesus for this valiant disciple and the opportunity you gave me to work with her side-by-side.

In 1991, the first fall we lived in southern Idaho I got a call from Carmen telling me that Mom was very ill and they were taking her to Missoula, Montana to the hospital. I made work arrangements and headed north. When I got there, they were taking Mom into gallbladder surgery. She was not in surgery long when the doctor came out and gave us grim news. After opening her up they found she was full of cancer. They just closed up the incision and placed her in a quiet room, knowing she would not last long. I sat beside her reading to her from the Bible. She had not woken since surgery and just lay sleeping. The second day as I was reading to her, she opened her eyes. I went to her and took her hand and ask her if she was ready to go Home. She shook her head "NO." I said Mommy are you ready to go Home to Jesus and Daddy, a small smile in the corner of her lip, her eyes brighten, and she nodded, "YES." She fell back into a coma and died the next day.

Her loss was wrenching to me. She had always believed in me, loved me, encouraged me, strengthened me. Oh God, how do I move on, what an enormous hole in my heart. Resting in Jesus, over time, I realized that the essence of my mother's strength dwelled inside of my soul. She has always been with me every moment of my life. Her death propelled me to give more to needy children. What would I have been without her great presence? How could I give some of those same qualities to the many children that have not had the privilege of a wonderful mother?

The next two years were marvelous. Jay graduated from high school and moved down to go to college in Boise. Bryce had served his three years and also moved to Boise to go to college. We fixed up an old shack behind our house into a bunkhouse for the boys to share. We had all five of our children in one area, life was constantly busy but very satisfying.

Living near the city gave me opportunities for further education. University of Idaho had a campus in Boise and I signed up for a Masters in School Administration. I was able to take night classes and finish this degree in two years. I also picked up my Special Education Administration certificate. I had finished one year of my doctoral program in Educational Leadership when our family life changed forever.

Chapter 8

The Accident
August 4, 1995

"Actually Mom, our relationship has been magnificent!"
Beth Smith

To him who overcomes and does my will to the end--I give him the morning star. Revelations 2:26-28 Christ is the morning star. It appears just before dawn, when the night is coldest and darkest. When the world is at its bleakest point. Christ will burst onto the scene, exposing evil with his light of truth and bringing his promised rewards.

Though Jim and I both confess Christ as our morning star, Beth's soul had star like qualities. Her open acceptance of all people, her generosity, integrity, morality, desire for peace and harmony, all these qualities allowed her star to shine in the darkest of days. I have pictures of Beth in her eight years as a quadriplegic, in constant pain, laughing so hard she lit the room. Her Spirit was so beyond the moment, the day, the week, the year. Though she must endure each day's physical limitations and constant pain, her inner strength shone through her indomitable Spirit. Her depth of Spirit caused her to live above all that. She lived in a selfless place that begged for harmony, peace and love. From the eye of an angel, she saw every ounce of goodness in each person.

I could tell Beth anything. She and I had an open honest relationship. I remember times when I was just tired and frustrated and would lie down beside her and pour out my heart. She had such a wonderful way of listening. She gave me her full attention and never interrupted. One time, one of the kids was driving me crazy and I was going on and on to her about this and that and she didn't say a word. I finally ran out of steam and waited for her reply and she just simply said, "He is always nice to me." Another time when I was at the end of my rope, of course you seem to take out your frustrations on the person you love the most and know will forgive you. So, this day I was going on to Beth about something Jim had said or done. I should have known better because Beth idolized her dad. I ranted and raved for quite some time. I leaned over her left side to hear her quiet voice and she said to me, "Have you kissed him today?" I said, "Beth haven't you been listening to me?" She affirmed that she had been and told me, "GO kiss my Dad." I turned to go do it and she called me back to her. Again, I leaned over her to hear her words and she said, "Kiss him like you mean it!" I turned again determined to follow her command, even though my heart was not in it at all. Still another time, she called me back and said, "Tell him you are sorry." I said "Sorry for what!" She interrupted and said, "It doesn't matter, go kiss him like you mean it and tell him you are sorry." Of course, by then I was no longer angry and able, with a sincere heart, go kiss my husband and tell him I was sorry. These are examples of how Beth ministered peace in our family.

The phone call came Friday, August 4, 1995, late in the afternoon. I was alone in the kitchen preparing dinner and Jim was working in the field. Answering the phone, I hear the voice on the other end saying, "This is the Idaho State Police." My heart sinks to the bottom of my chest. "Is this the James A. Smith and Kathy Sue Smith residence." Affirmative. "Do you own a late model red convertible Volkswagen." Oh God, I hear a piercing scream in my head and I drop to the floor. Yes. "Was a female driving this car." Jesus, Jesus – no – no, yes. I need you to come to St. Alphonsus Hospital immediately to identify said person." He quickly filled me in, there had been a head on collision and four people had been taken to the hospital. TOM- was one a young boy – Tom – he is twelve years old and was with his sister. Do you know where Tom is? He didn't know.

I opened the back door and scream for Jim; he comes running and through my shock and tears I repeat the conversation. We climb into the car and reach the hospital 30 minutes later. We had been instructed to go to the emergency room and check in at the desk. We are soon ushered into a cold, austere room, empty except for a gurney, with a body lying on it. Jim and I moved forward and as soon as I saw her baby toe, I knew it was my daughter, Beth. She was non-responsive, swollen to twice her size and was covered in blood. The moment we gave the nurse her vital statistics she was swept out of the room. We were instructed to go to the sixth floor, intensive care unit and wait in the waiting room. Wait! I say to the nurse as she turns to leave. Tom – where is our son Tom. Where is our baby boy – she doesn't know and tells us to wait in the emergency waiting room and she will make some phone calls. We wait and wait in the numb shocked state – speechless. My mind was racing. How could life change in 3 seconds? A police officer came over to us and asked us our names. "I'm sorry to tell you, your son was instantly killed in the accident." Where is he? Is he all alone? He is just a little boy. He's just a little boy! I fall on the floor screaming, he is just a little boy. I feel grief crawling up my back, lodging in my shoulders, causing extreme pain in my heart and my head. My sobs are wrenching and the pain so real I am sure I'm going to die and I don't care if I do. The officer and Jim help me up and we head upstairs to face the unknown about Beth.

Jim makes phone calls and within hours we have family and friends with us. The police officer that was first on the scene of the accident came to the intensive care waiting room to speak to Jim and I. He wanted to reassure us that Beth's accident was truly an accident. She was not driving impaired or too fast. The drive line on our car broke and caused the car to swerve into the other lane. She was simply, big sister taking her little brother to town to do his school shopping. He also informed us that the three passengers from the other car were all healing. His words were very comforting to us.

The doctors finally come out and list Beth's multiple injuries, lacerations, broken legs, broken neck and closed brain injury. She is in a coma but needs surgery to place rods in her broken legs, do a tracheotomy, and place a feeding tube in her stomach. Also, they are monitoring the pressure in her brain and if necessary, brain surgery to release the pressure. Her condition is critical and we are not allowed to see her the first 24 hours. The next morning her doctors say we can see her for 5 minutes. I was so terrified – I wanted to see her but she's all broken – my brother takes my arm and says, "Sue, you come from a long line of strong women. Hold your head up and let's go see Beth." I have never been able to erase the image of her laying in that bed. ventilator hose coming out of her neck, giving her breath - monitors – tubes – beeping, blinking instruments. Her long auburn hair sill crusted in old blood. But beyond all that was my daughter – my prayed for beautiful gift from God.

Jim's sister Diane stayed at the hospital to be close to Beth while we flew home to Carmen with Tommy. We were met by family and friends at the Salmon Air Port and taken to Dave's ranch on

Carmen Creek. My brother had his team of horses pulling a wagon and we placed Tom's coffin on the wagon and then all of his cousins climbed up and rode with him up to the family cemetery on the high bar of the ranch. Jim and I followed riding horseback. Hundreds of people came to send Tom home.

Tommy, Tommy, lover of life, you grew so strong in our family of love. We watched you, learned from you, and became so aware of the value of life. You saw things from such a pure, honest interested view. Your music was an expression of your joy in life, it came from the roots of your soul and shone through the dimples in your cheeks. Life to you was not a challenge, because you were good at everything. You could give and except love. Your heart touched everyone you were around. You thought school was a wonderful opportunity and enjoyed learning and friends. What you enjoyed most was family, and you knew how to make everyone feel happy and welcome. Tommy came to our home and extended family and friends to heal and become whole. Because of everyone's acceptance of Tommy, this was able to happen. Tommy is all better, he is strong, his heart sings, he is not afraid, and we give the gift we were given back to God. He lays on the high bar, where the sun casts its first light, the stars shine in abundance and the Bitterroot Mountains protect from the bitter winds.

Beth barely hung to life, we almost lost her

so many times. Swelling in the brain, high fevers, low temperatures, breathing issues, feeding tube infections. The amazing thing is life goes on – family head back to their homes – Jim goes back to work and day after day I head to the hospital. August turns to September to October to November to December and there is little change. She lies motionless. Her broken bones heal, her lacerations mend but her body stays asleep. It is no longer necessary for her to be in intensive care, so she is moved across town to the Elk's Rehabilitation Hospital. Doctors come and talk to us about the necessity of getting her off of the ventilator. They explain if we wait too long her body will not be able to breath on its own. They took the tube out of her tracheotomy for longer periods of time each day, within a week she was breathing on her own. Because she had never responded to touch, or sound the doctors had no idea of the extent of her brain damage.

Day after day I watched the nurses stir up this concoction of medications and pour it down Beth's feeding tube into her stomach. One night, in prayer, the Lord directed me to have the doctors stop giving Beth all her medications. I visited with Jim about this and we set up a meeting with her doctors. The doctors agreed, it was our choice to make this decision, letting us know the consequences could well be death. With more prayer Jim and I decided we had to follow the leading of the Lord. Four days after we stopped medication, I was up on Beth's bed doing range-of-motion with her arms and legs. As I was working, I watch Beth arch her back. This was the first movement she had made in over 6 months. All the days I spent with Beth I read her stories, visited about the family and sang her songs.

The next day her best friend, Dan Pokorney, came for a visit. They had been best friends through high school. We put Beth in her wheelchair and he took her out to the hospital garden. An hour later when he returned, he said, I think she understands." He had been visiting for weeks, and he could detect a difference in her demeanor. A couple of days later, again I am on her bed moving her arms and legs and I look up and she has opened her eyes. Oh, Beth, you are awake! I call Jim and go get the nurses. They call the doctors. She is unable to speak but she can answer yes/no question by blinking her eyes. Once for yes, and twice for no. You cannot imagine the relief and joy in that room. Six months in a deep coma, and little by little she is coming alive. A therapist brings an alphabet card and puts a wand in Beth's mouth. Very slowly she points to letters and spells, "W i l l s o m e o n e   p l e a s e   s c r a t c h   m y   n o s e ." Jim and I are ecstatic, not only does Beth have her intelligence she also has her sense of humor.

My next greatest concern was telling Beth about Tom's death before anyone else brought it up in conversation. Early the next morning as I pray all the way to the hospital, I enter her room. She's awake and I go to her side. Beth, I am so happy you are here with me. Dad and I have missed you so much and we will help you every way we can. She blinks to let me know she is hearing me. I have something I need to tell you, in the accident seven months ago Tommy died. She blinks again, and I can tell she wants to respond. I get the alphabet board and place the wand in her mouth. She points, "I already knew." How? "Gramma told me. She told me I had to come back to you." Remember my mother had died in 1991. I fell on my knees, thank you Mom and thank you Jesus.

Rehabilitation for a closed brain injury with quadriplegia is not for sissies. She had to learn how to swallow, hold her head up, speak, the list goes on and on. Hours of therapy every day for months and years. I am overjoyed when she is released from the hospital in April to come home. After a month of Jim and I doing 24-hour care we were both exhausted. We made the decision that Beth and I would move home to Carmen where we had family to help with her care, and Jim would follow in the fall. Beth slowly improved, learned to drive her electric wheel chair, was able to feed herself with an apparatus hooked to her wheel chair. At the time of her accident she was signed up to go to the University of Idaho and become a teacher or a counselor. As her health improved, she enrolled in Western Montana college in Dillon, Montana. We hired a care giver to live with her and she attended school for two years.

Even though God allowed me to have her, often times I was not satisfied that she was not completely healed. I would become angry and frustrated with God. In her second year of college she was up walking in a walker. She had worked so hard to get to this point. She was in college and really pushing herself on with life. She fell backward and hit her head hard. This led to a stream of 13 brain surgeries. The scar tissue in the ventricles of her brain would stop the flow of spinal fluid. Each surgery caused her to lose more and more function of her arms and legs. I took her to college after a weekend home and tucked her into bed; I turned off the light and lay down beside her on the floor. I stuck my head in my pillow and was silently screaming at God, I felt my heart was being ripped apart. Out of the stillness came Beth's voice. "Momma, we forgot to say our prayers." Beth said a beautiful prayer of thanksgiving, thanking God for her complete healing. You see, to Beth her body was nothing, her Spirit was complete and whole and because of this she could always rejoice.

Have you ever borrowed a tremendous, precious possession? You realize how very much the possessions means to the other person and so you treat it with care. Suppose you were in a very difficult situation and you had enormous decisions to make and you were not capable to make these decisions on your own. However, you had a friend, a very good friend that you trust and respect and this person has great wisdom. You go to your friend and you explain your situation and how desperate you are to borrow his wisdom for one month, knowing full well that as long as you have his wisdom, he will have none for himself. You take his wisdom and make wise, good decision; you prosper in knowledge and spirit. You go back to you friend and beg to have his wisdom just a little longer and your friend graciously grants you your wish. Time and again you go back to your friend and ask for an extension and many times you are given more time with his wisdom. Nevertheless, a day comes when you go to your friend and he tells you, "No, today I must take my wisdom back." Of course, you give the gift back with many thanks and leave your friend with assurance that you will give him the best of your abilities if he is ever in need.

June 18, 2003 Beth called me to her bed and told me it was time for her to go home to heaven, she said, "Please Momma, I want to go so badly." She said, "I am not giving up, but I am giving myself completely to God. I want to go off all my medication, no more hospitals and not more surgeries. Momma I know it is time for me to go." It was time for me to give back the precious gift I had borrowed. It was time for me to be full of joy and thanksgiving for all the beautiful times Beth and I had shared together. As I accepted Beth's decision, she and I had wonderful conversations about heaven. One day I said to her, Beth, we share the same Spirit and so I will always be with you and you will always be with me. And in her ever present, wonderful sense of humor she replied, "Then don't hang around any nasty kids," and then very seriously said, "Momma, our relationship has been magnificent."

Beth always wanted to be a minister, counselor or a teacher. Because of her health problems she was never able to finish for formal training. It wasn't until we let her friends and family know of her decision of no more treatment that the cards, letters and visits came in droves. After listening to her friend's thankfulness of her counsel and reading the lovely letters people sent, she and I realized she had been a minister, counselor and a teacher and taught and touched many people. This realization gave her a great deal of joy. Six weeks later she lay in the arms of her maker.

"What is the purpose of this suffering." Looking back, I believe Beth suffered for eight years for two reasons. First, I think God in his grace knew I would be unable to survive the death of two children at once. He allowed me time with my daughter, until I was strong enough to endure her loss. Second, this eight years enabled Christ to perfect His love in Beth's heart. To confirm a sense of confidence in her belief in her maker, to strengthen her in her fight against Satan and to establish her unchangeable foundation in Christ. Jim and I were able to witness this growth in Beth's Spirit. Her inner peace, her mischievous smile, her moral clarity, her empathy. Most of all her eagerness to witness and console those who were suffering. All of us wanted to emulate Beth's Spirit. Though she was the one in constant pain, though she was the one paralyzed, she was the light in the room. People were drawn to her flame, she would comfort, she would joke, she would voice the truth in her heart. Her greatest gift; was her ability to help people believe in themselves. Beth could pinpoint their talents, she would encourage and challenge them, and then delight in watching them grow.

Beth was laid to rest beside Tommy August 2, 2003. Words from Beth's Aunt Sylvia Smith. "After the funeral, I reflected upon the concept of "legacy." Beth's legacy is certainly one of love, humor, unwavering faith, and incredible courage. I thank you Jim and Sue, for bringing Beth into this world, and for instilling such beautiful beliefs and values in her. As time passes, I want you to know that Beth's legacy is important to me, and is one that I share with the special people in my life. I am sure that her legacy will give you strength even as you mourn her passing from this life. I feel as though I have been given a gift by being able to glimpse the legacy of this remarkable woman. I truly hope that you are able to find some comfort in these thoughts I share, as well the things that Beth shared with you over the years."

Chapter 9

Survival

Light obeyed, increased light:
Light resisted, bringeth night
Who shall give us power to choose
If the love of Light we lose.
Joseph Cook

Friends and family have asked me to write my story of surviving the death of our son Tom, and our daughter Beth. Actually, in a 12-year period of time I lost my mother, son, brother, and daughter. It is really not my story, but the story of my family. I guess it is my perspective, of our story. It is a story of everlasting love, tender, patient, enduring love, perhaps the deepest kind of love, love between a mother and her children. There are two reasons I have been reluctant to write. First, this story is very sad and I don't know if I have the strength to relive that portion of my life. Secondly, it is about triumph, it is about thanksgiving and it is about perfect peace... The story is about the long, long journey from extreme grief to triumphant peace. Even now as I sit in our cabin, twenty-four years since the accident, I feel anxiety fill my soul as I begin this story of survival.

I was so broken after we buried our second child. At first the sorrow was so enormous you feel you are going to break; your heart really does literally hurt. Jim would find me curled up in a ball, hiding in a closet, unable to face another day. As reality set in, I became like a hollow tube and then as time passed my heart turned to stone. I could hardly function. Everything took more effort than I had, getting dressed, brushing my teeth, making lunches. I was a broken person, shattered, crushed in a million pieces. I was helpless to know how or where to start to put the pieces back together. I knew I was broken on the inside; I just didn't know if I had the ability or strength to heal.

During this time Jim and I were in the mountains wandering aimlessly around. Heads hung low; hearts even lower as we search again for the perfect piece of granite to be used for our daughter's headstone. We finally decided on a rosy, peach colored, large stone that has fern lichens imprinted on it. The effort is made to dislodge the stone, load it in the truck and haul it to Boise to a carver. We explained to the stone carver exactly what we wanted on Beth's stone. He writes down the notes and takes our address. He then turns to us and says, "A few years ago I carved a stone for someone else from your town." Jim and I looked at each other. We didn't have it in us to explain, it was for our son Tom.

How do you hope when hope is shattered?
How do you call out when your soul is a vacuum?
How do you praise when oppression smothers
you?

I searched scripture for any clues on how to restore my shattered soul. In my study I became interested in the correlation between the Sprit, soul and the body. The Sprit of the Lord that lives in my heart gives me; wisdom, understanding, counsel, power, knowledge and respect of the Lord.

My soul is the power source of my,
(1) "mind; the collective conscience and unconscious processes that direct and influence mental and physical behavior."
(2) Emotions; "the mental state that arise spontaneously rather than through conscience effort and is often expressed in feelings of joy, sorrow, reverence, hate and love."
(3) Will; "the mental facility by which one deliberately chooses or decides upon a course of action." Free dictionary by Farlex.

The body consists of the physical body and the five senses.

If you cannot repair your shattered soul then the Spirit is empty. If you can't repair the shattered soul, then the body has no positive function.

With this knowledge I started analyzing my position. I recognized that my soul was broken. My mind would short-circuit, it would bounce around from one morbid thought to the next. I was ashamed of some of the things that went through my head. My will was destroyed. I could not make decisions. I could hardly decide what to wear. I knew I should be more involved with decision making for the family but I was simply unable to contribute. My emotions had bottomed out, nothing made me happy and nothing made me sadder. It was as if my emotions had nowhere to go, they were stuck. My soul was crushed.

I have always believed in God and even through all my loss I would feel His strength seep into me. But by the summer of 2003 I was losing touch. It was like the Spirit had dried up and was slowly, ever so slowly, dimming. My physical body was worn out. The essence of the body is the five senses but my body was so worn down I had little pleasure from any of my senses. I was a broken person body, soul and Spirit.

The Lord is near to the brokenhearted and saves those who are crushed in Spirit. Psalm 34

What is survival? My mind kept bouncing this thought around. Are you a true survivor if you have lived through a horrific ordeal and you are still alive? Are you a survivor if you are so maimed by the incident you are no longer functionable? Or is there more to being a true survivor? You live through the ordeal, but in time, you recover to the point where you can look back on this part of your life as a great growth in your person. I was asking myself, what destruction is unrepairable? Is my soul in a vegetative state? How do I become a true survivor of grief? The Lord's answer was, "Lean on Me, and on Jim and on the strength of your children and Christian friends. Serve your husband and children and rest in Me."

I really had two choices, get stuck in bitter grief and lose the value of my own life, and have my bitterness spread to my family and friends. Who wants to be around a grief ridden person, when they become angry, self-pitying, and have a negative force?

The second option is to value life and the love of the people around you and move forward, serving others and celebrating every joy possible.

I chose the second option, I chose life. However, I was in the pit, a deep dark well and could not even perceive of the possibility of Light. Each day I turned to God, each day I searched for answers. Each day I relied on Jim's strength, my children's council and encouragement from my Christian friends.

Jim came home one day and handed me the title to property he had bought, with Tommy's life insurance money, in the mountains above Salmon. This property was an old mining claim and in the same area I had spent my childhood moving cattle around the summer range. I was overwhelmed with gratitude, love and a sprinkle of hope. We drove up into the mountain to spend our first night on this God given piece of earth. I lay on the ground with my heart to the earth, I stretched my arms up above my head and dug my fingernails into the pine needles and the soil, I clutched them tightly into the palms of my hands. I whisper a prayer of restoration; I call upon the foundation of my heritage to instill in me the resolve to latch onto their roots, the root system is massive and strong, though I have been trampled and trod upon, like an Aspen, I have the ability to sprout again. By morning, I had gained enough strength to see a shimmer of light at the end of the tunnel. This was a healing place!

That winter we put up a wall tent and spent the winter months logging with our snowmobiles getting logs out to build a small cabin the next summer. It was a time of rest, reflection and precious healing. Sitting in the wall tent I wrote this letter to a dear friend. Greetings from Moose Creek. This morning as I was skiing up Diamond Creek meadow, I had one of the most profound spiritual experiences of my life. The perfect silence kept drawing me further on. I was skiing on top of three to four feet of cushioned snow. I entered a large portion of the meadow just as the sun crested the mountain and cascaded into the meadow. On the side of the meadow, nearest me, an enormous grove of bare aspen trees casting their shadows toward me. The sky was a pure ice blue with patches of soft fluffy clouds. I paused to completely grasp the beauty in front of me. Stopping, I realized the large pine in front of me is full of little red birds. The birds were singing a concert to their creator. My heart at this time was so full— God is still alive!!! I had no words to express the magnitude of His glory. The snow glistened like a million diamonds and I began to praise my creator. In my mind I could hear Jim's words, "A good marriage is like pure fresh snow, but ours has the extra glitter."

Lying on my back in a cushion of three or four feet of snow, staring up at the Lodge Pole, Douglass Fir, Blue Spruce that live together side by side in perfect harmony, off in the distance a grove of Aspen that have made their home in a moist area near a small meadow, the sky is an irresistible blue, the air crisp and cold, the silence deep and impregnable, the serene peace envelopes my soul. Yet lying there I become aware of the trauma that has passed through this very area of land. Mining has ripped and tore through this soil; high winds have sheared off innumerable trees and fire has left it completely desolate. The ability to revive, fight back against the odds, not only survive but exceed potential dreams and manifest itself in sublime beauty gives me a message of hope. Perhaps this is an analogy of what God has in mind for my life and yours. Death, sickness, poverty, joblessness, loneliness are all tools that have the ability to destroy our temporary stability in our walk, in life. However, if we take the time to reach up, the time to question, ponder, examine our innermost thoughts, hopes and abilities, we too have the endless potential to become substantially wiser, more efficient and productive with our time, more empathetic with a willingness to serve, and ultimately a stronger, deeper, more confident person within our inner selves.

I move forward one day at a time, each morning I fall on my knees and pray the Lord will show me how to serve Him, that day. One smile, one kind word, a hug or a job accomplished for the family. Serving others is the key to recovery and leads to deeper healing. Each time I hear news of someone losing a child I crumble to my knees; I can feel the intense pain of that mother. As time has moved on, I have been able to reach out to others who have suffered the loss of a child. A visit, a phone call, a reassuring smile. A bond is formed between us that has suffered this life event, a strength in each other's presence, a determination in our eyes, a pat on the back or hug that has mutual understanding. Our children will never be forgotten! Children are a mother's heartfelt gift from God. It is a mother's responsibility to nurture and care for their needs. It is God's right and privilege to call his children back home. I am thankful for all the gifts He has given me, and the time He has allowed me to be a part of their lives. I rest in peace accepting His timing.

When peace like a river attendeth my way,
When sorrows like sea billows roll,
Whatever my lot, Thou has taught me to say,
It is well, it is well with my soul.
It is well
With my soul
It is well, it is well with my soul.
Horatio Spafford

Chapter 10

Onward with God

As the deer pants for streams of water,
So my soul pants for you, O God
My soul thirsts for God,
For the living God.
Psalms 42:1

It is amazing to me looking back that even in the middle of our overtaxed life with Beth's infirmities, God continued to bring us children that needed a forever home. One day Jim and I were sitting in a Wendy's restaurant in Boise, Idaho, we were headed to Jerome, Idaho where Jim was doing an investigation. On the wall was a poster of Idaho children that were in need of homes. As we ate, we read about each of the children. We were both drawn to two brothers ages 5 and 7. They were African America with beautiful dark eyes. By the end of the meal we had decided to call the listed number and ask some questions about these boys. It was not a coincidence that these children lived in Jerome, Idaho right were Jim and I were headed. We ask the social worker if we could meet them.

In 1997 President Clinton signed into law the most sweeping changes to the nation's adoption and foster care system in nearly two years. The new legislation marks a fundamental shift in child welfare philosophy, away from a presumption that everything should be done to reunite children with their birth parents, even if the parents have been abusive. The legislation would instead give more weight to the child's health and safety. This law also allowed foster children to be adopted after they had been in the system for one year.

In 1997 we brought Ben and Sam home. They were as unsocialized as a barn cats, loud, wild, uneducated and malnourished. Ben was the oldest of 5 children and since he was three, he had been responsible for his siblings. He stole food, changed their diapers, tried to keep them warm and defended them, the best he could, from numerous boyfriends. When Sam came home, he had old cigarette burns all over his body. Ben was five years old when the children were removed from their home by Health and Welfare. Both Sam and Ben were lucky to be placed in good foster homes.

That fall we headed to the hills and set up a wall tent to spend a considerable amount of time. We were in desperate need to get these boy's behaviors in control. The wilderness gave up the opportunity to spend endless time with them. Each morning I gave them a school lesson and then their Dad taught them how to work getting in firewood and building fence. Over time, consistency, rock-a-byes and plenty of love they started to feel secure.

Sam really had an issue with food. He would get up at night and steal food and put it in his bed. It didn't seem to matter how I comforted him about the quantity of food at our home, he continued taking food. One day on the advice of Donna Velvick from Hope House I got an old pillow case and filled it up with healthy snack food and gave it to him. I told him when the food was gone to come to me and I would give him more. He carried this pillowcase with him everywhere he went for a year. Finally, I started seeing him leave it for periods of time, these periods got longer and longer until he no longer needed it.

Every month for many years I flew down to Hope House to help the teachers assimilate new students. I would test the students, work up lesson plans, train teachers and consult with Donna. That fall I was out on the playground watching the children play, I had been there often enough that I still knew most of the children. Out back behind the school I heard a little child crying and I ran back there to see what was wrong. A little tiny boy was holding his hand, large tears were rolling down his face. I did not know this little boy but I put out my arms and he ran to me, I lifted him up into my arms and he clung around my neck. When I got the tears subsided, I ask him if he were hurt and he held out his little hand. I could see that he had been bitten by an insect. I asked an older student nearby and she said a dragonfly had bitten him. I carried him up the steep stairs to Donna's office and we took care of the bite. Chris ran off to play and Donna asked me to stay. She told me Chris's terrible life story. He had been taken from his drug, alcohol mother at the age of two and placed in a foster home. The man in the foster home beat him with a broom handle and broke his skull to pieces. After a long stay in the hospital he was then put up for adoption. The adoption failed and he was brought to Hope House at the age of five. By this time Chris was filled with rage and anger. Donna had never placed one of her children out of Hope House but she asked Jim and I if we would take him. With Jim's background in psychology and counseling she felt we could help him. I called Jim and his usual answer, "Bring him home." Chris loved the mountains and the tent life. He and Sam became fast friends and played wonderfully together. Ben soon showed us he was a natural horseman, good in sports, played the piano and the guitar. Chris would go out in the pasture and just climb up on a gentle old horse and sit there for hours. I believe that horse fed comfort to Chris's soul. Chris was very involved with music both vocal and trumpet. Sam loved dogs. He would come home from school and head right for his dog.

The next year we get a phone call from Donna Velvick and she is asking Jim to do mediation. There was a little girl that had been left at Hope House but her adoptive father would not relinquish her rights. Donna thought that perhaps Jim could get this accomplished, so this little girl could move on with her life. I knew this little girl and had taught her in kindergarten. Jim agreed and started the mediation process. A year later the adoptive father relinquished his rights to Alex.

Alex was born to a single mother in California who gave Alex up for adoption, but it was to be an open adoption and she would be allowed to be a part of Alex's life. This worked for about a year and then the adoptive parents no longer allowed, Wendy, her mother to visit. Within the next couple of years this couple started having marital problems and the adoptive mother blamed their issues on Alex. This is what led to Alex being abandoned at Hope House. Later that winter, I receive a phone call from a little girl. She says, "Mrs. Smith, will you be my mother?" I turn to Beth who is in a bed in the living room and repeat the question to her. She says, "Tell her yes!" I talk it over with Jim and we bring home our third daughter. Alex was 10 years old and instantly is Beth's constant helper. She is so intuitive of Beth's needs. They spent endless hours listening to music, visiting and encouraging each other.

When Alex was 14 years old, we received a phone call from Alex's biological mother. She had been looking for her for years. Jim met with her and after hearing her story we decided to let her have visits with Alex. This led to Alex moving to California and living with her mother through high school. We are so thankful she had that time with her mother because her mother died of pancreatic cancer shortly after Alex graduated from high school.

We brought home one more boy, Zack, but he had severe oppositional defiant disorder. We were not able to help him assimilate into our home.

When Ben was in high school, he wrote this letter about his foster family and all they did for him.

"Since the first three years of my life is like stinky garbage, I choose not to take the lid off it very often. Though this garbage still exists, at five years old my life started to take on a new fragrance.

I have been charged with something I did not do. I was born into hell. My mom left me alone when I was two. She went out all the time. She used drugs and alcohol. Our house was like a garbage disposal. She always brought guys home when she was drunk. She thought they were cool but they were jerks to me and they stole things from her. Often there was no food in the house. She left me sick in bed. She would get back late at night. I was like a mouse looking for cheese. Like you leave some cheese out for a mouse. You sit there waiting for it and you fall asleep and you miss it. I was never able to get a hold of her for myself, she was never there for me. I have been left with a life-long sentence.

I found out what good was when I went to a foster home with Pam and Mike. They cleaned me up, had my haircut and gave me food and a nice warm bed to sleep in. I got to go to school. It was a good feeling to know I was going to have food when I needed it. I even had my first Christmas there. My foster sister had a baby and she taught me how to be nice to it. I was given a calf to take care of, I was shown how to care for it well.

I know my mom has goodness in her but she just couldn't see it. She cried when she came to see me. She would promise she would see me again. I hope she is in the AA getting help. Everybody has goodness; she just made bad choices. Bad can be reversed to good and make life seem better. We can still have bad fragrances but a good, new sense.

Ben

Ben is now in his tenth year as a marine, he is a staff Sargent and in charge of a platoon of young men. He was recently deployed to the middle east and while there wrote Jim and I this letter.

Dear Mom and Dad,

I hope you guys are well, I was giving a talk to some of my troubled marines the other day, and it got me to thinking about home. How little over ten years ago I was only a teenage boy sitting in my room looking out at the mountains and wondering where would my life be in ten years from then. I definitely did not envision I would still be in the marine corps, or even a father of three beautiful lives. Never did I see myself traveling the world as many times as I have, or how eager I was to leave Carmen, and the ranch. I have always found myself missing it all, working in the fields, rock picking, moving pipe, cows, haying, the whole package.

During this time of deployment, I have realized that you guys gave us a gift that cannot be bought, you and Dad gave us all the tools to be great leaders, whether we are in the military or working in a police department, a ranch or wherever it is. We take that work ethic that you guys taught us and apply it in that setting, so I want to thank you for adopting myself and Sam and the other children and giving us a better life and choices for the future.... Ben

Ben is a career military man with time spent in Special Forces. He is fluent in Arabic, Spanish and Japanese. He has three lovely children, and best of all, he is a great Dad.

Sam joined the Army after high school and was deployed to the 38th parallel. This is the division between North and South Korea. The tension and strain was more than he could handle and he was giving an honorable discharge. He has yet to recover completely and is living kind of an aimless life. I rest assured in Reverend Keele's words. "If Jesus has sunk a hook into a person, that person may fight up and down the stream, but eventually Jesus will bring him home."

Alex has moved back to Idaho and is very much a part of our lives. She is a senior in college getting degrees in sociology/criminology with a minor in criminal justice. Interestingly enough, this summer she is going back to Hope House to do an internship. She is a wonderful mother of a little girl.

Chris spent five years in the Marines and then went to school on his GI Bill. He studied sociology and graduated. He is now a city police officer in Lewiston, Idaho. He is married to a wonderful Christion woman and they are expecting their first child.

Bryce is married to Lynda Waldrop and they have two boys. Bryce is a detective in Canyon County, Idaho.

Jay is married to Chy and they have a son and two daughters. They are ranchers and live in the Carmen area.

Becky graduated from college with a degree in science and then got her Masters in lab-science. Isn't this astonishing, we were told she would never gain more than a third-grade education. She has now also finished a degree in elementary education and is teaching reading at a hearing school.

We don't often get all our kids' home at one time but we thrive on every visit we get. God's influence on these lives has been amazing to watch.

Pondering the past, thinking about the endless laundry, cooking, cleaning but more importantly the hours reading to my children, comforting them, rocking them, building a rapport that allowed us to communicate openly, I am so thankful for each moment. I thank God each day he allowed Jim and I to be the conduit that bridged these children to their maker. The Master's work has made their lives instruments of great value.

The Masters Touch
S. D. Gordon

"One morning a number of years ago in London a group of people had gathered in a small auction shop for an advertised sale of fine old antiques and curios. The auctioneer brought out an old blackened, dirty-looking violin. He said, "Ladies and gentlemen, here is a remarkable old instrument I have the great privilege of offering to you. It is a genuine Cremona, made by the famous Antonius Stradivarius himself. It is very rare, and worth its weight in gold. "What am I bid?" The people present looked at it critically. And some doubted the accuracy of the auctioneer's statement. They saw that it did not have the Stradivarius name cut in. And he explained that some of the earliest ones made did not have the name. And that some that had the name cut in were not genuine. But he could assure them that this was genuine. Still the buyers doubted and criticized, as buyers have always done. Five guineas in gold were bid, but no more. The

auctioneer perspired and pleaded. "It was ridiculous to think of selling such a rare violin for such a small sum," he said. But the bidding seemed hopelessly stuck there.

Meanwhile a man had entered the shop from the street. He was very tall and very slender, with very black hair, middle-aged, wearing a velvet coat. He walked up to the counter with a peculiar side-wise-step, and without noticing anybody in the shop picked up the violin, and was at once absorbed in it. He dusted it tenderly with his handkerchief, changed the tension of the strings, and held it up to his ear lingeringly as though hearing something. Then putting the end of it up in position he reached for the bow, while murmur ran through the little audience, "Paganini."

The bow seemed hardly to have touched the strings when such a soft exquisite note came out filling the shop, and holding the people spellbound. And as he played the listeners laughed for very delight, and then wept for the fullness of their emotion. The men's hats were off, and they all stood in rapt reverence, as though in a place of worship. He played upon their emotions as he played upon the old soil-begrimed violin.

By and by he stopped. And as they were released from the spell of the music the people began clamoring for the violin. "Fifty guineas," "sixty," "seventy," "eighty," they bid in hot haste. And at last it was knocked down to the famous player himself for one hundred guineas in gold, and that evening he held a vast audience of thousands breathless under the spell of the music he drew from the old, dirty, blackened, despised violin.

It was despised till the Master-player took possession: Its worth was not known. The Master's touch revealed the rare value, and brought out the hidden harmonies. He gave the doubted little instrument its true place of high honor before the multitude. May I say softly, some of us have been despising the worth of the man within. We have been bidding five guineas when the real value is immeasurably above that because of the Maker. Do not let us be underbidding God's workmanship.

The violin needed dusting, and readjustment of its strings before the music came. Shall we not each of us yield this rarest instrument, his own personality, to the Master's hand? There will be some changes needed, no doubt, as the Master-player takes hold. And then will go singing out of our persons and our lives, the rarest music of God, that shall enthrall and bring all within earshot to the Master-musician.

Chapter 11

Yoked

It is our business to study how we shall come into the midst of the purpose of God and have the unspeakable privilege in these few years of doing something of His work.
Phillips Brooks

Mathew 11:28-29 "**Come** unto Me all ye that labor and are heavy laden, I will give you rest. **Take** My yoke upon you, and learn of Me, for I am meek and lowly in heart; and ye shall find rest in your soul."

There are two invitations here, "Come" and "Take." To come is our invitation to salvation; life. The definition of salvation is the preservation or deliverance from harm or loss. Coming, believing in Christ is our first step, it is our guarantee of His daily presence in our lives and the reward of eternal life with Him. Unfortunately, I feel that many Christians stop at the "come" and overlook the next step, "Take." Take my yoke means daily working side by side with Jesus. It means recognizing Him as the superior being and being willing to submit to His authority. Yoking up with Jesus means a very close relationship, it means complete surrender to your Master. Always, there must be one dominate will, if there is to be power and success. He asks us to bend our strong wills to His, to yield our lives, our plans, our ambitions our friendships, our gold absolutely to His control," S. D. Gordon. The benefits to this yoking are a constant maturing in Christ. He teaches, directs, informs, counsels, encourages and most of all, is always there. We are never in the warfare of life alone.

This is not like a military command where surrender is forced. Jesus asks for only what we give freely and spontaneously. He does not want anything that is not given with a free, glad heart. Thankfully, I had the teaching, training and need to yoke up with my Heavenly Father many years ago. Because of this joint effort, working side by side with my Maker, most of my life has been filled with peace and harmony as I learned to listen, trust and obey His directions.

I don't know much about yokes on cattle but I know quite a bit about driving horses. Usually, you put a young resistive horse with an old seasoned steady going animal. The old worker sets the pace, and pulls evenly, steadily ahead. By and by the young undisciplined horse gradually comes to learn the pace. However, in the learning process there are times when the young horse tries to take the lead. When this happens, there are going to be some hard rides ahead, pulling back, sudden jerks, run-aways, and ultimate disaster. Then one gets to face the inevitable consequences. Life if full of webs and tangles, we can choose to go it alone, or we can choose to "Take," the yoke offered. I am so thankful for the forgiveness of my Heavenly Father, His constant and abiding love, his direction and steadfastness keep the yoke light.

Raising children that had been abused, abandoned, and neglected kept me daily in the yoke with Jesus. There was no way I could meet the emotional, social and academic needs of these children without his steady mentoring. Year by year, each in their own direction, they started leaving our home.

Standing in the empty room that our community had built for Beth and then we later used for the last five children we brought home, I find myself at the end of another chapter in my life. Am I ready for my next assignment? I spend days pondering, asking questions and seeking. It is early April and wild flowers of Lemhi, County are just starting to arrive. I catch my horse and head to the westside hill of the ranch. I am greeted with the first bluebells and yellow bells of the spring and next to them I spot of cushioned phlox. I peel off my horse and lay on the ground. How can God do this? We live in semi-arid desert and the hills are covered with sagebrush. We hardly ever get over 11 inches of rain in a year and our summers are hot and dry. And yet, each spring, these wonders appear, tiny, delicate, fresh and they fill all the gaps in my soul that have been doubting. Spirit fresh and new I head to my secret place to spend the day with God. By the end of the day I have heard once again from God:

"I want you to love me
I want you to be the best wife you can be
I want you to be the best mother you can be
I want you to be the best teacher you can be
I want you to start a charter school
I want you to teach reading
I want you to publish your reading program"

The love, wife, mother, teaching reading roles were in my comfort zone. Even starting a new school was not an overwhelming task because I had done it before. Writing an entire language arts curriculum for teaching reading sounded like a pretty big stretch for me. It was one of those "Really God," moments, are you sure you are talking to the right person. Flashbacks of my lack of skills in reading, writing and spelling started to throw doubts in my face. My mind was backtracking fast trying to justify why this was not a good idea, I could see failure all over it. In my panic I remembered the story of Jesus and Peter. This was before Peter had become a disciple. The story goes like this; Jesus was preaching to a crowd of people and they kept pushing Him closer and closer to the banks of the Sea of Galilee. He saw a couple men with boats not far away and He motioned to one man to bring his boat over. Peter brings the boat over and Jesus pushes off the shore and continues teaching the people. When He finishes, He motions for Peter to get in the boat. He tells him to push off to the deep and let down his nets. Now, Peter had been fishing all night long, he was tired and besides that, being a fisherman, he knew you could not catch fish in the middle of the day. Perhaps he hesitates deciding whether to explain all of this to the carpenter but decides to hold his council and lowers his nets. Low and behold the nets become so full of fish there is fear they will rip. The moral to the story is: listen to Jesus the master, trust Him and obey His command, the harvest will be greater than your wildest imagination can fathom.

Upper Carmen Charter School came into being in 2005. Beth's room turned into a classroom. The first year we had 24 student's kindergarten through third. This last year we had 60 students. The mission of the school is to develop each student to their greatest potential academically, socially and emotionally. Successful students emulate ethics of confidence, productivity and responsibility. A foundation of success in the primary grades sets the course for continued growth.

Upper Carmen flourished. In 2013 it was recognized as one of the top 5 rural charter school in the United States. In 2014 it was chosen as the charter school of the year in Idaho. The success of Upper Carmen Charter School is due to God's guidance, and the outstanding teachers that have taught here the last 14 years. This success has been followed by the opportunity and privilege for Jim and I to work with inspired people who are opening new charter schools throughout Idaho.

After the school was up and going, I turned my energies to writing my language arts/reading program. Learning to read was the most difficult task I have ever accomplished. In all honesty I did not become a fluent reader until I was grown with children of my own. This lack of reading skill was not because of lack of effort on my part or on my teachers or especially my mother. My dyslexia caused me to be unable to distinguish phonetic sounds one from another. During the 50's when I was in grade school, there was a heavy emphasis on sight word reading. Mom tried to help me with phonics, my teacher was using the sight word approach and I was stuck in the middle. By the time I was in 5th grade I considered myself the dumbest kid on the planet.

As often happens, we learn more if we have to struggle, by the time I had finished my Masters in Education I knew that I had been called to help children learn how to read. Each time I teach a child to read, and see the success in their eyes, I am filled with happiness. The BethTommy Read to Read method of reading was developed over twenty years. Now, I can see where God was coming from asking me to write and publish this program. First, my experiences of failure filled me with great empathy and compassion for children who struggle in learning to read. If by writing the

BethTommy program, I can help one child not have their self-worth destroyed by failure, it would be worth it. Second, God had given Jim and I, Becky. The training I received from the speech-Language Pathologist gave me a firm foundation of understanding language from first sounds to speech. Third, the ten years I spent at Hope House gave me rock solid experience in working with children that had lost everything. They had lost their self-worth, dignity, pride. They were broken children and God directed me through the steps to help them come alive.

I was amazed how closely God walked me through the writing process. I first wrote the curriculum. I was instructed, by Him, to incorporate all four learning modalities; visual (seeing), auditory (hearing), tactile (touching), and kinesthetic (moving). The purpose of doing this was to help children learn, who have different learning styles. As a dyslexic person, I knew one of the reasons I struggled, so hard, learning how to read was because almost all reading programs only use visual and auditory modalities. BethTommy uses visual, auditory, but also kinesthetic (sign language) and tactile (small plastic animals that represent each sound). The beauty of this program is the simplicity of it, how engaged the children are, and that magic moment when the abstract of letter/sound turns into meaningful reading.

BethTommy contains a step-by-step language arts program and two fiction books and one non-fiction book that teaches the basic phonetic rules in order to be able to decode the English language. Each story was a gift from God. I would know the letter/sounds I wanted to teach in the story and like magic the words for the story would be in my head. The downloads from God were so sweet and yet so humbling, I felt so privileged to be in His service. BethTommy was published in 2014.

I was a stay at home mom for twenty years, I was allowed the privilege of being there to nurture, love, and direct our ten children. I finished my first college degree when I was forty-one and have taught for 29 years. Because of my faith in God I have been granted the opportunity of teaching hundreds of children how to read. But better yet, I have taught young teachers the BethTommy method and to this day, schools around our state are using it to prevent students from ever having to feel failure. This is the wrap-around blessing of God; Becky, our deaf daughter, has been trained in BethTommy and teaches reading at Upper Carmen Charter School. I have been blessed.

As I write the last words of this book, excitement floods my soul, I know full well, that God is not finished with me yet. Once again, I will saddle my horse and head to the hills and visit with my Maker. What's next God, your servant is listening.

S. D. Gordon explains there is a very common delusion that holds us back from doing something because we are not skilled in doing it. We may be willing to "**come**" to the Master, we may even be willing to "**take**" up His yoke, but are we willing to "**serve**." Do we feel adequate, do we feel worthy, can we put, self, in its place and reach out to serve others?

Chapter 12

Acceptance

I will be glad in Your loving kindness, because You have seen my affliction.
Psalms 3:17

I started off saying this story is about a little girl with dyslexia. But really, isn't it a story about every little girl that perceives themselves different than whatever norm is? Couldn't this be a story of a little girl with a birthmark on her cheek, a little girl in a wheel chair, an abandoned, deaf little girl or an emotionally rejected little girl. It is a story of our internal anguish, the pressure we encounter from the outside world, the hard work of always swimming upstream to fit – to belong – to be recognized. It is the constant external drive, we place upon ourselves, to set high goals. To exceed admirably in the sight of others, constantly hiding, always on the alert, expecting to be found out. Continually trying to prove to ourselves, we are acceptable, we are adequate and we are worthy

The trail He gave me to ride had rough narrow passages, steep peaks, along with gentle slopes. But really, isn't that life. Perhaps I am not so different, perhaps everyone has their own disability and their own trails to navigate.

As I look back on the trail of my life, I have come to a point of realizing I should be thanking God for my disability and my inadequacies. These are the things that have kept me dependent on God. My successes in life came by the direction of God and my desire to be obedient to Him. To God be the glory. My disability is exactly what made me fall on my face before my Lord. However, my dependence on God was yet another one of my secrets. I needed Him to fill my lonely heart – I needed hope and love and for sure I needed guidance and direction. In my eyes the rest of my extended family were perfect. They were smart, independent and self-sufficient. To my immature understanding, I needed God because I was not smart and certainly not self-sufficient. To let other people, see the light of Jesus shine through me, would be like opening the door to my scared heart. I would be exposed, people would see the real me, the me, I so desperately tried to hide. In my naivety, I did not know you cannot hide the love of Jesus, it shines through your eyes, it is extended by your heart, it reaches your smile or is known by your actions.

Today, I have come to a point in my Christian walk where I can fully surrender to Jesus. I am ready to open up all the closed, hidden areas in my heart. It is time to lay, "my all" at the feet of Jesus. By doing this I feel clean, inside and out, I am at perfect peace with my maker. I now understand I was not a mistake; I was formed perfectly in God's sight. I will always be dyslexic, but I am no longer ashamed of my dyslexia. Overcoming the limitations of my disability by holding God's hand has been the key to my satisfying successful life. Being able to thank God for something I spent a lifetime hiding. That is a giant step.

The greatest spiritual blessing we receive is when we come to the knowledge that we are destitute. Until we get there, our Lord is powerless. He can do nothing for us as long as we think we are sufficient in and of ourselves. As long as we are "rich," particularly in the areas of pride and independence, God can do nothing for us. It is only when we get hungry spiritually that we receive the Holy Spirit.
Oswald Chambers

My prayer is that the God of our Lord Jesus Christ, the Father of glory, may give to you a spirit of wisdom and of revelation in the knowledge of Him. I pray the eyes of your heart may be enlightened, so that you may know what is the hope of His calling, what are the riches of the glory of His inheritance in the saints, and what is the surpassing greatness of His power toward us who believe. Ephesians 1:17-19

Recently, Jim and I headed to Arizona to camp in the desert. A time for togetherness, reflection and thanksgiving. While we were there, we listened to a Charles Stanley sermon on solitude. I have always spent a great deal of time with the Lord but honestly, I have done far more talking and not near enough listening. So, I wandered out into the desert to get in tune with God. I had recently retired and had been pondering what is next in my life. God has never left me idle. But I know from experience that you better be prepared before you ask him what is next. I felt His pull in my heart and I fall on my knees in the sand. O.K. Lord, today I am just going to listen. The words of Longfellow enter my mind, "Let us then labor for an inward stillness—An inward stillness and an inward healing; That perfect silence where the lips and heart are still, and we no longer entertain our own imperfect thoughts and vain opinions, but God alone speaks to us, and we wait in singleness of heart, that we may know His will, and do that only." The sun was on my back, the desert stretching endlessly in front of me and I pull my mind to nothingness. I have no idea how long I was there absorbed in His love. Then I hear: "I want you to love Me." I stay still and He repeats himself: "I want you to love me." I look down at the dried-out sand, the surface is cracked and the many pieces form an uneven design. Slowly it comes to me, these are the pieces of my life. The rough, jagged pieces of my shattered soul. "I want you to tell your story." I have come to the point in my life that when God asks me to do something, He is really asking "us" to do something. Though I am fully aware of my limitations, He is fully aware of my potential. He is simply asking for my obedience. It is not a short story; it took a lifetime.

The Lord starting picking up pieces of my shattered soul. One piece at a time, He would smooth the edges, sand the splintered surface and teach me about love. He would pick up the next piece, whittle off the rough edges, and teach me about joy. Piece by piece, year by year He taught me about peace, patience, kindness, goodness, faithfulness, gentleness and self-control. Then, he took those pieces and made a frame for my life. He continued to fill in the puzzle, one piece at a time, teaching me about everlasting love, acceptance and adequacy. Then he took up the final piece and fitted it perfectly into the center of the puzzle and shared with me, "This is a picture of your victorious life." Because I learned to love the Lord, he turned my weaknesses into strengths. Strengths that have given me a victorious life but better yet, strengths that have touched others.

Epilogue

When I am an Old Horsewoman
Patty Barnhart

When I am an old horsewoman, I shall wear
turquoise and diamonds,
And a straw hat that doesn't suit me
And I shall spend my social security on white
wine and carrots,
And sit in my alleyway of my barn
And listen to my horse breathe.
I will sneak out in the middle of a summer
night
And ride my old bay mare,
Across the moon struck meadow, if my old
bones will allow
And when people come to call, I will smile
and nod
As I walk past the gardens to the barn
I'll show stalls fresh-lined with straw.
I will shovel and sweat and wear hay in my
hair as if it were a jewel
And I will be an embarrassment to all
Who will not yet have found the peace in
being free, to have a horse as a best friend
A friend who waits at midnight hour
With muzzle and nicker and patient eye
For the kind of woman I will be
When I am old.

At the end of my last trail, I'll swing off my horse, and build my last campfire. I will lie on my back and quietly gazing up at the stars. I'll see the heavens open up and I'll say, "It's been a great ride Lord, thanks for never letting me ride alone." I hear His loving voice speak to me:

"I want you to love Me".
"I Do."
"I Have."
"I will.

Made in the USA
Middletown, DE
31 January 2020

84007292R00099